God Goes To Dark Places

Copyrights

Foreword

Jihya's journey through fire has transformed her into the extraordinary woman of faith, love, and strength I am honored to call my wife. Her story is not for the faint of heart, but it will not fail to inspire those who read it to draw closer to our Lord, Jesus Christ, through the lens of forgiveness and grace. As you read about the hardships she's endured, you may find yourself wondering how anyone could move forward without bitterness or anger. And truthfully, few would deny her the right to hold onto those feelings after so much pain. What sets Jihya apart is not only her refusal to do that—but the way she chose forgiveness, again and again, as the only path to true healing through the power of the Father.

I have had the pleasure and privilege of being Jihya's husband for nearly a decade, and I've witnessed many of the resounding victories and painful setbacks captured in this book. Some chapters were especially hard to read, particularly the ones recounting the abuse she endured. As her husband, knowing that someone I love so profoundly went through such darkness is heartbreaking beyond words. There were moments I had to pause, not because of disbelief, but because of how honest and raw the pain felt due to her expert emotional writing, even these many years later. And yet, even in those darkest moments, what shines through is not just the horror of what happened but the incredible strength it took to survive and the even greater strength it took to forgive and heal.

Hearing her story, then and now, is sometimes devastating, but more than anything, it is a testament to transformation. The young woman who began in rebellion is now the beloved daughter of the King I had the joy of marrying. Her heart is to love people right where they are, without condemnation or judgment, and to extend the healing love and hope that only God can offer and the love she has experienced firsthand.

At its core, this book is about redemption. It's about love that survives and thrives, even when the world has given you every reason to shut down. Jihya's journey will especially speak to those who have walked through trauma, broken relationships, abuse, sexual sin, and even wounds inflicted by those in the church itself. Sadly, these experiences are not uncommon. But in Jihya's story, they are not the final word. They are not what defines her.

What the enemy meant for evil, the Lord has indeed turned to good. Her life and ministry are proof that God never forgets His children. He will leave the ninety-nine to search the deepest darkness for the one and use anyone to carry His light.

I invite you to step into this story—into the pain, heartache, and suffering—with the full assurance that redemption is real and healing is possible. Jihya will sweep you along with her honest, powerful storytelling and remind you that no matter where you've been, hope and God are never out of reach.

M. Tobias Harris, *Jihya's husband and author of Echoes of the Tomb*

To women in dark places, God goes to you.

Table of Contents

Glossary

Korean Words

Appa – Father
Umma – Mother
Halmeoni – Grandmother
Gomo – Aunt (on the paternal side)
Han – A deep, often unspoken sorrow, lament, and grief
Bop – A bowl of rice
Kimchi – Spicy and sour fermented cabbage, a staple in Korean cuisine
Jjigae – A comforting, spicy stew, often made with tofu or meat
Gashina – A southeastern Busan slang word that can mean young woman or baby girl

Selah

Throughout this book, each chapter will end with the Hebrew word *selah*. In scripture, it is a pause or interlude, often in a song or poem. Selah invites us to pause, reflect, and meditate on the truth. It's a moment of stillness, allowing words to sink in and resonate with the soul.

Perhaps something in my story echoes your own journey. When that happens, let it be an invitation to pause — to linger in the moment, reflect on what you have read, and make space for God to meet you right where you are. I encourage you to take some deep, intentional breaths. Let the words settle, let your heart respond, and allow the Spirit to gently stir within you.

These pauses are sacred. Use them to reflect, pray, and be present. Each chapter includes a suggested scripture or quote to guide your reflection and help you feel closer to God's presence.

Disclaimer

Please be advised of the explicit and sensitive nature of certain subjects shared throughout the book. Be aware of your own triggering responses that may be evoked. Names and locations have been changed for privacy and protection.

1

Running Away

It was a beautiful sunny day. As I waited outside for my cab, I looked up at the sky. Not a single cloud in sight; a rarity for most days in Southern California.

Another picturesque day. Yet, my life and this moment were anything but perfect. Everything was shattered, fractured into pieces beyond repair.

Once again, I found myself running away from another toxic, abusive relationship. I thought marriage would be different, but it wasn't. I was a broken person. And, completely *helpless*.

There were a few hours left before he would return from work. I couldn't bear being here any longer, couldn't endure the sight of the home we had made together, built on lies and deception. Our shared belongings, once symbols of a life we had dreamed of, now made me regret and feel repulsed.

The cab pulled up, and I climbed in quickly, clutching a small duffel bag to my chest like a lifeline. It contained the only things of value I had left. It had my wallet, some cash I'd saved over the past five months, a small toiletry bag, my favorite clothes to last me a few days, and the only mementos I cherished: pictures of my childhood; reminders of a simpler time before all of this.

That's it. Nothing more.

This small bag was my only possession and was now my sole comfort.

As the cab drove away, a strange peace began to settle over me, a salve to the wounds I'd been carrying. I allowed myself to dream, just for a moment, of a new future.

A new life.

A second chance.

A fresh start.

It felt distant, but it was there. I was one step closer to a life without him, a life where I could find myself again.

The driver didn't speak. There was silence between us that stretched on. I stared out the window, lost in thought, but I could feel his eyes on me, his gaze flickering back to me in the rearview mirror.

He was an older man, dressed in faded flannel and denim overalls. He reminded me of the farm workers from the Midwest, where I grew up.

Could he tell? Could he see that I was running away, that I was escaping something I couldn't speak of?

I tried to avoid his gaze, feeling a pang of discomfort each time his eyes met mine. He seemed on the verge of saying something, but never did. His body language was tense, his hands gripping the wheel with seemingly an unnecessary amount of force.

The peace I'd felt earlier began to fade, and anxiety crept back into my chest. The doubts returned, racing through my mind and body. I could feel my heart begin hammering in my chest, and before I knew it, tears began to fall, hot and unexpected, streaking down my cheeks.

I couldn't stop them.

It was the same cycle each time I left. Doubts, guilt, the temptation to turn back, to believe that maybe, just maybe, things could change. He could change. Or maybe I could change.

I wondered if I could ever go back and pretend that everything was okay. We could try again. We could rebuild our lives together and find happiness. We could forgive and forget what happened in the past.

But I knew.

Enough was enough.

I had finally reached my breaking point.

The outbursts.

The rage.

The lies.

The accusations.

The broken promises.

The shattered furniture.

Finding my personal items in the ocean where he had thrown them. The endless cycles of breaking up and getting back together.

I was 20 years old and my options felt limited. I could stay in this marriage or leave.

But leaving meant being alone. It meant uncertainty. It meant facing a world that didn't feel safe, possibly living on the streets.

Several weeks earlier, I'd passed by a gentlemen's club, and an idea had surfaced, one I pushed away and dismissed. I couldn't be a stripper. I couldn't take off my clothes for a living. Growing up, I was told women like that were trash, broken, drug addicts, and unworthy.

I couldn't be one of them.

The thought of my family, my Korean family, being ashamed of me brought heartache. What would they think? I couldn't bring more dishonor to them. I couldn't live with that.

There was another option: I could call Appa and ask for help. However, my pride wouldn't allow it. I couldn't take his hard-earned money to cover my mistakes. Not again.

I couldn't go back to the Midwest—there was too much pain there.

So, here I was alone: 1,600 miles away from my family.

The idea of working at the gentlemen's club pulled at me. It offered freedom and independence. Something I'd never had before. I'd always been dependent on men, but this would be different.

I told myself I'd work there temporarily, just long enough to save for my own place and car. Then, I'd return to waitressing and even go to college like I dreamed.

The cab pulled up to the gentlemen's club. The driver turned to me and spoke for the first time, "Are you sure this is where you want to be? Are you sure you want to go in there?"

His questions stopped me. It was as if he were warning me, urging me to reconsider.

I felt like I was at a crossroads, standing on the precipice of a decision that would define my identity and future.

After meeting his eyes and holding his gaze, I answered with a steady voice, "Yes. **Yes, this is where I want to be.**" The moment I said those words, something shifted inside me.

A surge of *empowerment.*

A sense of *control.*

Stepping out of the cab, I stood in front of the gentlemen's club. The flashing neon lights above the entrance seemed to pulse with a strange energy. The door was dark, but inviting.

I was afraid, but there was a curiosity too, a magnetic pull. Something inside me was aware that my old life, as I knew it, was over.

There was no turning back.

I reached for the handle.

And with that simple gesture, I entered a place I never could have imagined — a world of deception and broken dreams where people come hungry and have desires. A world that would change everything for me. A world where I would lose myself, and in the process, find pieces of myself I never knew existed.

Not yet knowing that this very place would be where one day Jesus would come for me — *to save and show me He loves me.*

Selah

"For the Son of Man came to seek and to save the lost."
Luke 19:10, ESV

2

Gentlemen's Club

It was a bad night. It was Saturday and hardly anyone was spending money. The customers reeked of alcohol, some drunk as early as 8 pm. Their slurred speech, unsteady gait, and fuzzy memory was obviously noticeable especially when it came to paying the dancers.

This was a typical weekend at the gentlemen's club where I worked. Here, everyone was welcome as long as they were paying. The strip club was open 7 days a week, 365 days a year, from 11 a.m. to 2 a.m., even on holidays like Thanksgiving and Christmas. A business, where adults of all backgrounds and classes came to be entertained by pretty women — women who danced naked on stage, offering lap dances for extra pay. Some customers came on their lunch breaks, others after a long day at work, and some, like tonight, came to celebrate bachelor parties.

But tonight? Tonight was different.

These men weren't here to spend. They were here to spectate, gawk, and sometimes harass, especially after too many drinks.

It was one of those nights where every dancer had to be on high alert, even with more bouncers on the floor. The club had seen some turnover in the security staff, but the current bouncers were good. They cared about the dancers' safety. They ensured that the customers followed the rules and didn't cross the line especially when they got too handsy or drunk.

Tonight, there was a darker presence in the air, an "icky", sickening feeling. The requests from customers were crass and degrading. We were reduced to shiny objects, dehumanized by both men and women alike.

A bachelor party was coming in — a group of guys, eager and rowdy. They burst into the club laughing hysterically, high-fiving each other. It was clear this was their first time at a strip club. Their eyes were wide and their mouths were watering. They were mesmerized by the sight of a naked girl twirling on a pole.

They waved dollar bills in the air, thinking it would somehow impress us. Some of the newer dancers might have fallen for it, but most of us, seasoned by nights like this, didn't bother.

For me, bachelor parties were always a no-go. I couldn't fake being nice just to further objectify myself. These guys assumed that just because we were dancers, we had no boundaries, that we'd accept any request, even the disrespectful ones.

The requests were worse when they offered drugs or alcohol to entice us to join them after our shifts, or worse, tried to get our phone numbers to "keep the party going." The thought made my stomach churn.

Inside the club, things were controlled. There were rules. But once the dancers left the club, things could get dangerous. Street workers, escorts — anything outside the club was a different world. I heard the cops didn't come to the aid of these girls because it involved sex work.

I had always been uneasy around large groups of men, tiptoeing around them, hoping they wouldn't notice me. If it was a big client, especially one the club was loyal to, I was expected to serve them, whether I wanted to or not. Sometimes they would want one of each type of girl, a token for every race and body type. Tonight, I was that token. The Asian girl for the bachelor party. I couldn't escape them, not without raising suspicions.

Sighing heavily, I thought to myself, this was going to be a long night.

Stepping into the dressing room, completely drained from everything that had happened on the floor. The chaotic energy of the club had worn me thin — the flickering lights, blaring music, drunken customers, and more catcalling than usual. It was overwhelming to say the least.

"I just turned down a couple who wanted to 'spice up' their marriage," Starlight complained, plopping down next to me.

Starlight was one of the few people I trusted in the club. A petite, 5'1" Black girl, we were the same age and both transplants to Southern California. On the outside, she appeared tough and determined. Sometimes people mistook her for being angry. She'd jokingly say she was ready to fight anyone who tried to take her down. Beneath that tough exterior was a tender heart, one that cared deeply for others, especially animals. She dreamed of owning enough land to raise every kind of livestock.

Starlight had a wild backstory, one that often shocked people. She'd been in foster care, suffered abuse, and when she turned the legal age, her foster parents dropped her off on a street corner just a few blocks away from a strip club. That was how she ended up working in the adult entertainment industry.

When I asked her about her past, she'd always start with, "It's a long story, but in a nutshell..." and tell me the whole story of how her dad had been wrongfully accused of murder and locked away when she was only five. She hadn't seen him until much later in life, when she visited him in prison.

Her mom had lost custody when she was ten years old due to alcohol and financial instability. Similarly to me, she had a story of survival, and in this world, survival meant building a new future driven by hustle for the ability to make ends meet.

"They wanted a discount. They 'only' had $10. Can they not read the sign? Lap dances on the floor are $20!" Starlight vented.

"Eff that! Giving dances to couples is so draining," I replied, rolling my eyes. "Why don't they spend that on marriage counseling instead?"

"He tried to argue that it didn't count for his wife because she was a woman. What does that even mean? I don't discriminate. The price is the same for both men and women! He insisted and even raised his voice at me. I should have told Beef and gotten them kicked out, but the husband said he'd find another girl who'd be willing. Ugh! I HATE COUPLES," Starlight vented.

I laughed, half-joking. "Damn. That would be me, I said. Honestly, though, I'd rather deal with a couple than some drunk guy acting like an idiot. I just wanted to go home. Tonight SUCKED.

Glancing at my reflection in the mirror, I hated how nights like this made me feel.

Weekend nights at the club were always rough and tempted me to numb with alcohol, but I swore I'd never drink at work. It broke one of the rules I had set for myself when I started this job. Another was never to give out my real name or personal details. This was not a place to make personal connections. I couldn't risk losing control, especially because it was to make a living.

Five more dances in the VIP room, then I could finally leave. I could go home.

I took a deep breath and sighed. I walked out of the dressing room.

Selah

"I am with you always." *Matthew 28:20, NIV*

3
Exit Plan

My new one-bedroom apartment was barely furnished. It had been nearly six months. I was used to living this way in survival mode, keeping things light in case I had to move again. I never had a permanent home, so I was used to moving from place to place.

I was hardly home, only there to sleep and get ready for the club. Most nights, I was either working or partying. This was normal. This was part of the price I paid for my lifestyle.

In the darkness of my one-bedroom apartment, I sat alone and thought about a way out — an exit plan to leave the adult entertainment industry.

At twenty-four, I thought I was "adulting". The most important thing in my life at the time was that I had earned my own car and secured my apartment. I could afford things. Even though I wasn't making an honest living, I was finally free from abuse. When I first started dancing, I told myself I would do it for only a year — just until I got settled, until I was on my feet.

But weeks turned into months, and months into years. Five years later, I found myself stuck in the same place, with nothing to show for it. Sure, I had traveled abroad and bought expensive things, but I hadn't earned the college degree I promised myself I would. I had nothing that I could openly be proud of.

After the first year, the novelty and glamour of dancing wore off, replaced by a harsh reality. I felt trapped, physically unwell. My knees were bruised, and my body ached from the work. My relationship with my family was already broken and had grown more distant. I didn't have any real close friends. The longer I stayed in the industry, the more I lost sight of what truly mattered.

I hadn't told anyone I was dancing to make a living. It was my secret. I wasn't about to admit it, let alone explain it.

One evening, as I sat at my small dining table, I reached under a pile of junk mail and grabbed my notebook. I began to list all my living expenses, big ones like rent, car payment, phone bill, and groceries. I penciled in the cost next to each. As I calculated, I realized that if I were frugal, I could get by with about a thousand dollars a month.

It was nothing compared to what I was making, but it could be enough to help me leave the club.

Could I really leave?

I thought about my best months, how I had made $10,000 in one month, and how I could make even more if I wanted to. But that would require me to sell more of my soul.

How much more of myself could I trade for money?

For the first time, I felt a glimmer of hope, a possibility of a way out. Immediately, an intrusive thought scolded. It was loud, accusatory, and relentless.

Where else can you make that kind of money?

Who would hire you with a gap in your employment?

The weight of those questions pressed down on me.

How would I explain my past to a future employer?

What could I say?

Who could I put down as a reference?

There was no way I was going to list the strip club as my current employer.

I tried to ignore the thoughts and keep pushing forward, but every time I scrolled through online job postings and read their required qualifications, I started to believe the lies.

The hope I'd felt began to fade, and my dreams slipped away. This was my life, and I believed that there was no future for me beyond the club.

Selah

> "I have it all planned out. Plans to take care of you, not abandon you, plans to give you the future you hope for." *Jeremiah 29:11, The Message*

4
Between Two Worlds

When I was a child, I was imaginative and free-spirited. I found wonder in the simplest things, like large picture books and wild dandelions. I marveled at them, fascinated by their colors, shapes, and beauty.

After school, I would spend hours riding my bike, feeling the wind glide through my hair. I loved being outdoors.

My bike wasn't like the other kids' bikes. It had a long, banana-shaped seat and lacked the bright tassels hanging from the handlebars. It was plain, but it was mine, and I loved it. People would often look at it with disdain, but I didn't care. If only they knew how fast it could go and where it could take me.

I would ride for hours, singing Mariah Carey songs as I sped down 31st Street with the sun slowly setting until Halmeoni called me home for dinner.

Summers in the Midwest were scorching, with triple-digit temperatures but evenings would bring some relief. On particularly humid nights, flashes of light would appear in our yard; my signal to go back outside.

Those golden embers were lightning bugs. Their soft, yellow glow magically illuminated the night. Though tiny, they seemed to carry an unseen strength. It was comforting, a gentle reminder that someone, perhaps a higher power, was watching over me.

They'd float around me; their tiny sparks dancing. If one landed on my shirt, I'd carefully scoop it up and let it crawl on my palm, admiring its delicate beauty.

As with the little bugs, my childhood was simple. But I didn't have flashy clothes or fancy toys. I didn't know we were poor or had less education. But as I grew older, I realized how different my upbringing was from my friends'. They had Disneyland trips, piano lessons, and family outings. I didn't have those things, but I felt secure that I had everything I needed, even when my family was just scraping by.

Koreans in the Midwest stood out. We were seen as foreign and exotic. We were called oriental. It never felt welcoming. At the grocery store or mall, people would stare and make comments, often about how we smelled. Was it the kimchi on our breath? The jjigae or sesame oil stains on our clothes? Or maybe it was just the secondhand clothes we wore?

I didn't understand what being an immigrant meant. When I read "resident alien" on my green card, I honestly thought it meant I was from another planet. There was hardly anyone else with straight black hair and almond-shaped eyes like mine. When people spoke to us, their voices would slow and their gestures became exaggerated, especially when Appa and Halmeoni were around.

Sometimes, I would respond in perfect English, hoping to make them stop treating us differently. Then they would stare at me and expect me to translate and explain for them. Eventually, I grew tired and embarrassed, and I stopped wanting to run errands with Appa.

At home, I longed for time alone, but it was impossible in a house full of immigrants. I often felt misunderstood, like no one really knew me. In my narrow, childlike worldview, I thought I was the only one who truly understood myself.

In many Asian households, words like "I love you" are rarely spoken. Love is shown through actions. Mine was no exception. We were reminded of love through an extra serving of rice in our bowl or when someone asked, "Did you eat?" It wasn't just a question — it was a sign of care, a daily mission to make sure we were always full. When relatives came from Korea, they brought gifts such as socks and little accessories for everyone. It was their way of saying, "I thought of you." Food, gifts, and acts of service were how we expressed love in my family without words.

During my elementary school years, I preferred being alone to being around others. I was shy, quiet and self-conscious about my language skills. There were sounds in English that were so different from the Korean spoken at home. Every week, I dreaded the speech lessons I was pulled out of class to attend.

At times, I felt invisible. Other times, I felt completely exposed. Some kids ignored me, while others were curious.

One day, a girl with big blue eyes and shiny yellow hair asked, "Where are you from?"

I swear, she looked like she stepped right out of *Goldilocks and the Three Bears*.

"Here," I shyly replied.

"No, like, where are you REALLY from?" she asked, her eyes wide with a kind of daring curiosity.

My nervousness grew, and my face flushed bright red. But there was no way to hide my embarrassment. It was playtime in the classroom, and with all the kids around, it felt as though a spotlight was shining down on me. All eyes turned toward me, and I was stuck in the middle.

I didn't know what to say. The truth wasn't simple. It was complicated, and explaining it felt like a long, painful process. I dreaded the series of questions that would follow. I was afraid of what they might think of me or my family. I was terrified of telling them that I didn't have a mother. I feared they'd think something was wrong with me, that I wasn't lovable.

Kids can be cruel. We already got strange looks at the grocery store, now school would be another setting to feel out of place.

Frozen in place, I couldn't speak. But before I could answer, the girl said, "Are you from China?"

Another kid nearby overheard and repeated the words loudly, "China! She's from China! China girl!"

I stood there, motionless, my heart racing, in a strange mix of shock and relief. Shocked that they had assumed I was Chinese when I wasn't. But, oddly, I was relieved that I didn't have to explain my real story. That truth hurt too much.

For the rest of elementary school, I was known as "China girl." People assumed my family was Chinese. I never bothered correcting them. It felt safer to let them believe a lie than to share the painful truth.

The real story — the story of where I was born and the reasons why we left had caused so much pain and changed the course of my life, and of those I loved. The story that planted the seeds of feeling unworthy and unlovable.

Selah

> "But now, O Jacob, listen to the Lord who created you. O Israel, the one who formed you says, 'Do not be afraid, for I have ransomed you. I have called you by name; you are mine.'" *Isaiah 43:1, NLT*

5
Busan

Busan, a vibrant city on the southeastern coast of South Korea's peninsula, was my birthplace. The city's rich history, stunning landscapes, fresh seafood, and unique flavors fill the air with a welcoming warmth. To the north and west, it is surrounded by low-lying mountains, while the southern and eastern borders are defined by the vast ocean. Buddhist temples are perched on steep cliffs, and sandy beaches stretch out before them.

As I grew older, I would occasionally catch glimpses in pictures of places I visited as a child. However, the more I tried to recall those very early memories, the more they slipped away, clouded by time and distorted by lingering trauma and grief. The deeper I reached into my past, the more elusive they became, like trying to grab at mist in the early morning. It was as if a barrier had been built in my mind, preventing me from fully accessing these memories.

The memories I was able to hold onto became dear to me. They only dated back to when I was about five years old, and these remained close to my heart. I would cherish them, but some I longed to run from as well, especially when they resurfaced unexpectedly, bringing with them a wave of sadness and despair.

To this day, I try to sort through these memories, questioning whether this jumble of images was real or imagined. But there was always a feeling deep within me, a quiet certainty that these memories were as tangible and true as the objects I can touch in the present.

While I did not have the word for it as a child, my empathy was more attuned than that of my peers. I could sense the sorrow in the people and places around me. Perhaps this was *Han*, the collective grief that runs through the hearts of many Koreans—a grief born from decades of colonization, war, and unresolved trauma that continues to haunt the country's collective spirit.

Some of my earliest memories in America involve visiting the public library and searching through travel books for images of Busan, hoping to find visual confirmation of the places I remembered. After studying these pictures closely, I would compare them to the images in my mind, searching for validation that the memories were real and that I hadn't simply imagined them.

In those library photographs, I was always drawn to the mountains. Was this the reason I've always felt a deep connection to mountains whenever I saw pictures, or that when I got older, I enjoyed hiking so much? Is it merely a coincidence, or is it possible that we inherit certain inclinations, certain callings, deep within us from our first breath?

Just as certain sounds and mannerisms are naturally ingrained in the voices and bodies of Koreans, I wonder if some things are encoded in our very DNA by our designer —traits that shape who we are, things that go beyond explanation. These are not just memories; they are instincts, woven into the fabric of our being by God.

Selah

> "I knew you before I formed you in your mother's womb. Before you were born, I set you apart and appointed you as my prophet to the nations." *Jeremiah 1:5, NLT*

6

Rebellious Nature & Family Secret

The jagged boulders looked like elbows sticking out of the
ocean. The strong waves came crashing forcibly, one after
another, moving quickly. I vividly remember how they crashed
up against the boulders, making big splashes. The waves were
unmerciful and swept the ocean water without ceasing.

A little tinge of fear crawled up my spine, but I shook it off.

Although I was small, I believed I was immeasurably big.
Believing I possessed a special power, I pretended I was
invincible. I was out to test my boundaries.

I don't remember Umma ever being around, but graciously,
Appa was. He was always there in my flashbacks of this part of
my childhood.

Climbing on one rock then another to get to the top, I imagined
my hands and feet were much bigger than they actually were. I
climbed using every muscle as if they were a sturdy anchor that
kept me from falling into the bottomless sea. Appa insisted that
I get down from the rocks and be careful. Still, I ignored him
and pretended not to hear his instructions.

Finally, I made it to the tallest and last boulder. Feeling
accomplished, I turned back to see how far I had come. I could
see Appa in the distance. Despite knowing that I had
completely rebelled and disobeyed my father, I still smiled and
waved proudly, showing off what I considered to be a great
achievement. However, Appa was frustrated, and it showed on
his face. I could still make out the words under his breath, the
word he often referred to me as: *gashina*, a southeastern Busan
slang that refers to "baby girl". This time, it didn't sound

endearing like it normally does. Rather, it made me feel ashamed, and I started to regret my actions as I made my way back to him.

When I was little, I had always wanted to ask Appa what happened between him and Umma. However, early on, I had internalized the unspoken message to never bring it up because it would make him depressed. Therefore, I never asked.

I didn't want to make Appa sad. I respected my father very much, and he never deserted us like our mom did. I remember vaguely hearing about how he had a chance to stay in Korea and only send his children to America. Or take us to an orphanage. But, neither of these options could he accept. He chose to stay with his children and be a single father when he had an opportunity to leave us.

So, whenever I questioned whether he prized me or not, when he wasn't around because he had to work such long hours to provide for us, I would remind myself of his losses, both in Korea and America. Acknowledging his sacrifices on my behalf kept me from becoming bitter towards him. I wanted to know what happened between my parents, but as I got older, I shied away from making any inquiries, and the real narrative got pushed further to the back burner.

It wasn't helpful that whenever we talked about the past or someone asked a question, there was a shudder of silence. It would require a superhero's power to muster the courage to sit through some of our family conversations, sifting through the multi-faceted levels of pain, fear, and confusion—layers held down by shame and generational trauma.

As I grew older, no matter how much time passed, the ponderings remained locked in the attic of my mind. Contemplating the "Whys" of my past only brought out the same monologue in my subconscious – Will I ever know the truth? Maybe some stories aren't meant to be told or known.

I have never heard their story directly from my parents. It always seemed taboo. A family secret.

But, behind closed doors and in conversations shared privately, this tale was whispered outside of our family —

They were young.

And in love.

They had a family quickly.

The father worked long hours while the mother stayed at home caring for the children.

After having their last child, the mother had trouble bonding with them.

Caring had become burdensome. Too much for anyone to manage alone.

She needed help, but no one knew it was what she needed.

The neighbors were concerned and had serious questions about what was going on in that home.

They kept a close eye and stopped by regularly, because sadly, it was common to find the children at home alone without any supervision.

Where was the mother, people thought?

They were worried.

In the town nearby, there were rumors circulating that she had become crazy and that was the reason for her hospitalizations.

Others said she got involved with a religious cult.

She was having auditory hallucinations, hearing demonic voices.

No one really knew what was going on inside that home. Or how to help this young couple.

As time passed, it was clear their marriage was failing and their home was further falling apart.

More trouble awaited in that home, and their children were at risk.

When the townspeople talked about that family, everyone feared.

Shame and cultural etiquette made people keep a distance.

It would be impolite to get involved in someone else's business, especially when it comes to private family matters.

Then in the quiet hours of the night, she left.

Vanished. Gone.

There was no goodbye.

No letter of explanation for her choice.

There was no request for her children or belongings.

Or a fight for them.

No signs that she was taken against her will.

In their home, she leaves behind the man and children she once loved.

And, instantly, all their lives are changed—forever.

Selah

> "I promise that I will never leave you helpless or abandon you as orphans—I will come back to you!" *John 14:18, TPT*

7
Where Love Begins

Life begins with a love story....or so I thought.

As a mother-baby nurse, I have witnessed and heard countless birth stories. Some are ideal, filled with joy and anticipation; others, less so. In my work as a registered nurse, I've seen how birth, while often romanticized, isn't always the fairytale it's made out to be. Every birth story has a unique narrative of love, loss, and everything in between.

For most, the retelling of their birth story means hearing about the love they were born into — marked by the date and time, hospital details, inked prints of tiny feet, and those precious first moments. Excitement fills the room as visitors arrive with balloons, gifts, and food to celebrate the new life. Joy permeates as memories are captured during a baby's first feed, swaddle, and showing of expressions. In these moments, love feels tangible and everything seems perfect.

But not all stories unfold this way.

Sometimes a birth story may involve a mother's sense of loss because the birth plan didn't go as expected.

Sometimes, it's a story of forced adoption, escape from domestic violence, or entrapment in addiction.

Sometimes, there is pain with breastfeeding, or the disappointment of the baby father's absence.

Sometimes, the story is of a baby's fight to stay alive during their own withdrawal because of the choices made for them by the mother.

These are the stories that don't often get told.

When I hear birth stories like these, I can't help but relate because my own story is far from perfect.

Newborn footprints, photos of me being welcomed by my parents, or even a birth certificate are not part of my story. I was born outside of the United States at home, a place with different customs and standards. However, regardless of the story, traditions, or customs, there should be one universal truth that binds all births together: love.

Unfortunately, before I came to know Jesus, I did not feel loved. Not because I didn't know what love was, but because I felt its absence. My story began with a painful absence, which is where the lie of being unlovable originated. I didn't feel worthy of love because the beginning of my life made me believe something was terribly wrong with me.

That burden stayed with me for years, far longer than it needed to.

The simple truth is, I don't remember my mother. Family members tell me she left when I was a baby. There were no pictures of her in our home, so I have no memory of what she looked like. I never knew her name or birthdate. To this day, I have never received a letter or a gift from her. Not even a phone call to let me know she was thinking of me.

Growing up, I wondered if it would have been better to have a mother who was just absent sometimes, like my friends whose parents were divorced. Or was her permanent absence actually a blessing?

When people asked me, "Where's your mom?" I would make something up like, "She's on a trip to Korea." Even though I hated lying, I hated pity even more. Somehow, it felt safer to fabricate a half-truth than to let anyone know how deeply I longed for her.

The truth was too painful! Explaining that my mother's absence was her choice was too much to bear. I could not tell them that she left me; that she didn't want me. It was easier to imagine I wasn't even born from a mother at all. Maybe I grew inside a petri dish within a lab. It was a better fantasy than the truth of abandonment.

Even though my mother wasn't around, I was fortunate to have other mother figures in my life. My Halmeoni and Gomos on my father's side were a constant source of love and support. But there was still an ache in my heart, a longing I couldn't ignore. It wasn't until I was older, at sleepovers, that I saw a different kind of love—a mother's love—a love that was intimate, tender, and affectionate.

I first saw this love when my friend's mother tucked her into bed. She swept her daughter's hair away from her face, kissed her forehead, and lovingly whispered, "I love you. Sweet dreams." It stung deeply because I realized that kind of love was something I'd never known, something I had longed for but never received from my birth mother.

As I grew older, the pain did not fade. It only grew, especially on Mother's Day, when I was reminded of the love I never received. Even after I became a Christian and forgave my mother, the ache remained. It crept in on occasions that should have been joyful—my wedding day and the births of my own children.

The questions lingered: *Where is she? How could she walk out on me? What would my life have been like with her in it if she hadn't left?*

I rejected anyone who tried to offer me a mother's love, even the people who had the best of intentions. The lies I told myself were convincing. Lies such as: I will not be fit to be a mother myself.

The stories told about my own mother's struggles with mental illness after having me only reinforced the lies. The enemy planted thoughts in me that if I became a mother, I would be just like her: unfit and broken. Not wanting to repeat that generational cycle, I resolved to never have children.

Then I became a mother.

In the thick of postpartum depression, sleep deprivation, and struggling to adjust to my new identity and routine, those same taunting accusations flooded back in.

YOU'RE UNQUALIFIED.

YOU'RE UNFIT.

YOU'LL NEVER BE ENOUGH FOR YOUR CHILD.

There were times when I wanted to run away and abandon my family. I would think of bridges and entertain jumping off. I wanted to escape the overwhelming weight of it all. However, in those darkest hours, Jesus and my husband were there with me. They held onto me, they fought for my life, and reminded me of the love that had been missing from my story. They spoke words of truth:

You are qualified.

You are fit.

You are enough for your child.

Selah

"For you created my inmost being; you knit me together in my mother's womb. I praise you because I am fearfully and wonderfully made; your works are wonderful, I know that full well." *Psalm 139:13-14, NIV*

8

The Boogeyman

Many parts of my story felt too dirty to share publicly. However, being silent only made the torture grow stronger. Suffering the hidden pain became too much to bear alone.

For years, I kept this chapter of my story buried beneath layers of shame and silence. I convinced myself that if I ignored it, maybe it would disappear. Maybe it didn't really happen.

I assumed I had to protect others from knowing, feeling uncomfortable, or thinking less of me. But in doing so, I carried the burden alone. I tried to suppress the memories, pushing them so far down that they became distorted. I told myself they weren't real. But trauma does not vanish — it festers. When it surfaced, it manifested in ways I could not control.

Intimacy was a struggle; I recoiled from touch and disassociated from my own body. It was as if I had an open wound that had never been cleaned, and thus it became infected, rotting beneath the surface. Though there were many moments when I could have faced it, I just wasn't ready.

Numbing was easier.

Detaching was safer.

Ignoring was simpler.

You might be thinking what happened?

I was **molested**.

Even typing the word molested makes my skin crawl. For years, the idea of saying it out loud was unthinkable.

The memories are murky. I can't remember exactly when, but I believe I was around eight years old when it began.

It happened on and off.

At that age, I did not have the language to explain what was happening. I didn't know how to process it either. That it wasn't my fault; that I didn't deserve it. It would take years, well into adulthood, for me to connect the dots, to understand that I had been groomed when I was a child. But despite my young mind's inability to fully comprehend, my body knew it was being violated.

Waking up to soiled sheets, I had begun wetting the bed at night, my body's way of screaming out for help. However, instead of recognizing it as a response to trauma, I felt humiliated. I started hiding the sheets, too ashamed to let anyone see. I further blamed myself.

Why didn't I fight back? Why didn't I scream? Why didn't I run away? Was I broken? Was something in me defective? Did I deserve it?

These were the thoughts that materialized in my mind over and over. I believed them.

At school, I overheard kids talking about a terrifying figure. They called him the Boogeyman. A monster that came after bad children. I was sure he was coming for me. He lived in my neighborhood, but he didn't look like a monster. He didn't hide in the shadows. This boogeyman was clean-cut, charming, and polite. He waved at everyone who passed his house. He knew people's names and asked how they were doing. A good neighbor. Or so people thought.

One summer afternoon, I was pedaling my bike past his house and caught him staring at me. It was one of those moments where I wasn't supposed to notice, but I did. He smiled. I looked the other way, my heart racing. My gut told me to avoid that street, even if it meant taking a longer route.

Then one day, as I rode to the park, he was there.

"Hey," he said, jogging toward me. "Are you the girl who lives in the house with the trailer parked out front?"

I nodded hesitantly.

"I'm John." He extended his hand for a handshake.

I shrunk.

"I just finished my run. Can I walk you home?"

Not wanting to be rude, I nodded again.

Most of what he said that day, I've forgotten. He asked me about school, what I liked, and what I didn't. He wasn't that scary up close, maybe because he talked about things I understood. He was acting like he cared. When we reached my driveway, he waved goodbye and jogged away. I was relieved and confused. He didn't act like the monster I had imagined him to be after all.

For weeks, I didn't see him. His garage door stayed closed. The usual signs of his presence — the running sprinklers or garden tools left outside were gone. Maybe he moved. Then one day, he was back. His garage door was open, and he was standing there. A part of me felt excited; a part of me felt strange for feeling that way. Did I have a crush on him?

No. No way!

That thought made me feel a way that I hadn't experienced.

Later that day, I rode my bike past his house.

"Hey," I said.

"Hi." He smiled. "Did you have a good day at school?"

I only nodded as I had no intention of staying any longer. But before I could leave, he asked, "Do you want to help me move something inside?"

Hesitating because I didn't want to be rude. "Um... sure." I pushed my bike into his garage, laying it down on the floor next to a large crate.

"Are you getting a dog?" I asked.

"Thinking about it," he said. "I always wanted one to go running or hunting."

We lifted the crate together, carrying it into his house. Once we got inside, I noticed how empty it was. There were no pictures or decorations. The walls were starkly bare. There was only a couch and a lamp in the corner. This did not look or feel like a normal home.

"Well, I'd better go," I said.

"Thanks for your help," he said.

Then, after a pause, he slowly asked, "Do you know how pretty you are?"

I froze. Suddenly feeling uneasy.

I had never had anyone tell me that before. My face turned scarlet from embarrassment. How could I feel so uncomfortable and flattered at the same time? I quickly realized I shouldn't be here and turned to leave.

Before I could reach the door, he placed his hand on my shoulder, and my body stiffened. He stepped *closer*.

Standing still, I was unsure of what to do. He pressed his body against mine and leaned into my hair, breathing me in. Then he kissed my neck. I stiffened and couldn't move. If I stayed rigid, maybe he would stop. But he didn't stop. His hands moved lower down my pants. Then I felt something I had never felt before. Everything turned **black.**

There was no light. Darkness engulfed me.

I wanted to cry, but no tears came. So, I whimpered for help on the outside while I shrieked inside my head. Yet, I had no voice.

No one heard me, and no one saw me. That was the day I lost my voice and innocence.

Friend Request (13 years later)

A 'Facebook Friend request' popped in from Ryan McCallum.

Is this really the Ryan I knew from my childhood?

It had been over a decade since we last saw each other.

Ryan was a year older than me and lived near 31st street. He was quiet and had a reputation of being the skater kid in my neighborhood. We were only acquaintances and occasionally passed each other on bikes and skateboards. There had been some rumors that he was held back for poor behavior. He always appeared disheveled and kept to himself.

I clicked 'Accept'.

Instantly, I received a message in a chat from him.

We initiated some small talk about basic stuff like where we live now and what we are currently doing. We mused over our childhood. We quickly went down memory lane reminiscing about the park with the old tire swing and laughed out loud about how many kids suffered a concussion from falling off it, including ourselves. Then we couldn't forget to mention the creepy creek that separated the park from nearby houses; how it was the favorite place to hide as kids.

Out of nowhere, Ryan typed, "Remember the tan house?"

As I read "the tan house," I froze.

"Hope that creep isn't still living there. He's probably rotting away."

My heart started racing and I panicked. It felt like my secret was out. Exposed. Does Ryan know?

Resisting the urge to confess, but having no control, I type, "What creep?"

There was a long pause. I could see he was typing, stopping, and then re-typing. Typing again and finally stopping. No words came on the screen, but a bubble appeared and then disappeared. After a few long minutes, he typed, "Can we talk on the phone?"

Something didn't feel right. I knew it was serious and my stomach began to spasm. I looked at the time and realized I had to head for a class I was taking at the community college. My response was a quick text, "I gotta get ready for class. Maybe tomorrow?"

He proceeded to type, "Sure. It's nothing. We'll talk sometime."

"No, I REALLY want to chat. I think we should. I just can't miss this class again. Sorry."

"Yah. Here's my number."

All afternoon, my mind was racing and restless. The resurrection of memories from the tomb in my heart, where I had long ago buried them, was excruciating. It took one mention of a tan house to bring the flashbacks to the surface of my conscience.

During my class, I couldn't concentrate and walked out without excusing myself.

As I got into my car, I started sobbing. I knew the creep Ryan was talking about, and I knew what evil made him a creep.

The next day, when I was supposed to call Ryan, fear held me back. I didn't want to talk about the tan house. The house where I was sexually abused. I felt taken advantage of and guilt-ridden, but mostly dirty. I avoided calling him for a few days, but couldn't stop pondering and wondering what he had to say about the "creep." Conflicting inner voices chanted, "If anything, it's probably nothing. I'm sure it's nothing. I'm just overreacting." So I just pressed my anxious misgivings deeper and ignored them.

The next day, I finally mustered the courage to call him. While it rang, I kept wishing he wouldn't answer and just let it go to voicemail. After the fifth ring, he did answer, and my heart groaned.

"Hello."

"Hey Ryan, it's Jihya."

"I know," he scoffs. "I didn't think you would ever call, but I'm glad you did."

We talked for over three hours. He confided that he was molested in the tan house. He thinks there may have been other children involved, too.

Although I was shocked, I was also relieved, because I didn't feel isolated and alone anymore. I was also outraged. How could he have done this to Ryan and possibly another child? When he changed the subject, the words, "He did it to me too," spilled out of my mouth.

Then everything else came spewing out like vomit. My body was trying to purge the wickedness that had festered for so long. It felt as if I had entered a vortex, with a vacuum sucking out every filthy detail. I told him everything from when it began until the last incident. I couldn't stop because, for the first time, it felt safe to confide in someone.

Hearing the words outside my body sounded horrifying, but simultaneously liberating. A heavyweight fell from me.

"Ryan, are you still there?" I asked, hearing muffled sounds in the background and him cursing under his breath. He apologized for what happened to me, to us. We stayed on the phone for some time without exchanging any words. There was a mutual understanding of what we both were experiencing and facing.

Then curiously, I asked, "Do you know if he's still around?"

He proceeded to tell me that he looked him up online a year ago and couldn't find him. There wasn't a trace of him on the internet. So, Ryan went to the old house and knocked on the front door, not knowing what to expect. It had been sold several years before, and the new owner had no information on him.

Ryan was mired in the past, while I had moved on and learned to suppress the pain. Ryan was full of rage and sought vengeance. I could hear the bitter anger in the tone of his voice, and I understood. My empathy for him allowed me to see the ways he had been so deeply hurt; they were similar, yet very different from how we processed pain.

He was a disheveled kid, but there was always a light about him. Sadly, that light had dimmed from the abuse. Ryan grew up and, like me, moved out of state to work in construction while picking up a few shifts at a bar. Most nights, he would revel in drinking and partying. He was endeavoring to cope with his agony.

Slowly, I began sharing with him some of my aspirations to go into journalism, and I had begun taking college courses at a community college. What I couldn't share with him was that I stripped to make a living and pay for school. He would look at me differently.

In fact, I told no one what I did for a living. If people knew how much I earned as a stripper, they would be disgusted. Therefore, I would avoid talking about what I did. I had become good at living a double life.

Yet I was convinced this was the only way to live.

Selah

> "The light shines in the darkness, and the darkness has not overcome it." *John 1:5, ESV*

9
Suicide Attempt

The new man in my life wouldn't answer my phone calls.

The phone kept ringing, but it went straight to voicemail. I heard the abrupt click, but knew he was aware of my calls and deliberately disregarding them.

Once again, I felt ignored and abandoned.

Just like the last time, and the time before that. He wasn't there for me when I needed him most, even though he said he would be.

He told me that he could not be with someone who took their clothes off for a living. Yet, would still show up now and then, telling me he cherished me, but his actions didn't match his words. How could someone say they cared and wanted to be with me, but couldn't because of my job?

I assumed he understood my reasons. I thought he was on my side.

Was he ashamed of me? Embarrassed by what I did?

Again, I explained that this was temporary, that stripping was just a stepping stone to get me where I wanted to be. It was helping me become independent and had freed me from my last relationship. It put food on the table and gave me a roof over my head. Without the club, I would probably be homeless, unable to survive, let alone pursue my goals.

Still, his actions were demeaning. They made me feel rejected and unworthy of love.

I tried calling him again. And again. This time, the phone didn't even ring. It went straight to voicemail.

I was spiraling out of control.

My thoughts were loud and piercing.

Anxiety gripped me, and dejection clenched my heart.

I wanted the throbbing pain to stop.

I felt misunderstood.

No one sees me. Or sees the good in me.

All they see is a stripper.

Everyone wants something from me.

I hate this.

I hate myself.

I don't want to live.

I should just die.

That thought held weight.

The more I contemplated it, the more tempting it became. It clung to me like static, comforting me in its darkness. Its shallow presence wrapped itself around my mind, luring me into its depths.

I reached for the bottle of Jägermeister in my cabinet. I remembered the pills — pills I had gotten at a party, still in the bottom of my bag.

Opening the prescription bottle, I swallowed the pills and chased them down with Jäger.

Gulp, gulp, gulp.

I downed the entire bottle.

Immediately, I realized what I had done. It wasn't intentional, but it was too late. My vision blurred, my senses dulled. My body felt light, as though I was floating into a bottomless, dark cavern.

I lowered myself gently onto the cold kitchen tile, feeling my pain slowly disappear and feeling a hollow emptiness surrounding me.

The darkness pulled me in, while the familiar voices of shame and regret taunted me.

Tears began to drip down my face, and I realized — this was the biggest mistake of my life.

In that moment, I whispered, "God, I'm sorry. Please forgive me."

And then, I slipped into a deep, abysmal sleep.

Miracles

My memory was fuzzy.

I don't know who called 911. Or how I was transported to the hospital.

I had overdosed and blacked out. I don't remember the ride in the ambulance or the IV being put in.

But I do remember waking up to the soft sound of prayers. They were faint at first, but I could make out a few words. As I regained consciousness, I felt an overwhelming sense of supernatural peace.

There was a comforting presence, and I heard a woman's voice clearly, *"My child, I'm so glad you're here. Praise Jesus for your life."*

Was she talking to me? If so, I didn't deserve her kindness. After all, I had just tried to take my own life. Was this a dream? Maybe she hadn't read my chart yet.

I opened my eyes and saw a woman beside me.

"Hello, my name is Marisol. I am your nurse."

Marisol was radiant, with a warm, almost angelic demeanor about her. She was a beautiful older Filipino lady, her hair neatly pinned up in a bun. Her bronze skin seemed to glow, as if freshly kissed by the sun. She wore a navy blue cardigan over a white scrub dress and wedge shoes. Her gentle composure and pristine attire gave her a peaceful, caring presence.

I was safe with her. Nurse Marisol made me feel truly seen. She was compassionate and caring. She stayed with me for most of the day, providing comfort until early afternoon when she had to hand me off to another nurse.

This new nurse didn't introduce herself. She explained nothing. She was distant, cold, and silent as she removed my EKG leads and IV. She handed me a fresh gown and instructed me to change. Unlike the first gown, this one had faded stripes and no ties in the back, like a slip-on dress.

I thought she would leave to give me some privacy, but instead, she stood by the door, arms crossed, eyes sharp. She watched me as if I were a specimen, judging me without a word.

There was a chip on her shoulder that reduced me to being despicable. I could feel it, a palpable distance between us. She didn't trust me and certainly didn't care to get to know me. She looked at me like I was trash to be discarded.

"Okay, I need your hair tie and your socks," she demanded. I removed the hair tie from my tangled hair and took off the socks. Nervously, I asked, "Do you know where I'm going?"

Without even glancing up, her face unreadable, she barked, "5 East. The psych unit."

By 5 p.m., I was in a single private room. There was no curtain separating me from the rest of the unit, just a bed, a toilet in the corner, and a small window near the ceiling. It was solitary confinement. No alarms from monitors or IV pumps. No footsteps or voices outside my door.

Surprisingly, it was peaceful.

The unexpected result was that my mind functioned clearer than it had in days. I was away from all the noise of the outside world and protected by these hospital walls. There was no pressure, no demand, only routine and rules. Unrecognized at the time my soul craved the order and boundaries this place offered. I had never realized how much I needed that sense of structure.

As I lay there, the sunlight streamed through the small window and touched the foot of my hospital bed. The warmth was comforting. Nurse Marisol's words came back, and I let their peacefulness wash over me. They felt full of life and compassion in contrast to the harsh words I had grown accustomed to in my daily life.

Beneath my messy hair and the gown I wore, covered in the remnants of my brokenness, she had seen me. She saw more than the mistakes I made.

I couldn't help but wonder about the person she praised. And who was she talking to? Was it God? The same God I had heard of in the Catholic church when I was younger, the God who seemed so distant, so unreachable? The God who required perfection to be loved? The God who had a strict set of rules.

How could a God like that accept me? How could He forgive me for what I had done to myself, for everything I had done in my life?

How could God allow something like this to happen if He was truly God?

Tears began to well up, and an unfamiliar weight of guilt pressed in. For the first time, I felt convicted. Not ashamed or embarrassed, but truly convicted.

The tears kept coming. I didn't hold them back like I normally do.

I whispered, "God, I'm so sorry."

And in that instant, something changed. Deep inside, I felt a sense of forgiveness. Just like that. I knew, without a doubt, that this was the last time I would try to take my life. I would never overdose again.

The next morning, I was discharged from the hospital. It was

Sunday. The hospital gave me a taxi voucher, and I was dropped off at my apartment. My cell phone was on the kitchen counter with a few missed calls from friends. No one knew where I had been, or what had happened to me.

Although I was glad to be back in my apartment, the space seemed hollow and empty. Barren. I picked up the mess from the night before and sat on the couch, unsure of what to do next.

There was nothing important or meaningful left in my life.

Most Sundays, I would continue the weekend's cycle of partying. A few girlfriends from the club would meet at a beach bar, but now the thought of alcohol disgusted me. I knew it was time to change.

I recalled driving by a large church a few weeks prior. The signs outside read, "Everyone is welcome" and "Come as you are." It was just after 10 a.m., and I realized I could make it to the 11 a.m. service if I hurried, so I quickly got ready.

Walking into the church building, I gaped at the grand entryway. Inside, it was even more spacious, with a main auditorium and a balcony. I took the stairs to the second floor and followed the sound of the worship music. Taking a seat in the fourth row, near the back. I could see the entire room, filled with people worshiping. Some were standing, hands raised, others on their knees in prayer. They were all moving with the rhythm of the music.

The lead singer, a large Black woman, sang with a voice that came from her soul. As the music slowed and faded, she spoke into the microphone, "*My child*, I'm so glad you're here. Praise Jesus for your life."

I was stunned. Baffled, to say the least. Those were the **exact words** Nurse Marisol had said. Had she known I would be here? Was she somehow friends with the singer? How did she know to speak those words?

A hundred thoughts raced through my mind. I couldn't stop rationalizing it, telling myself it was just a coincidence even though my heart told me otherwise. Maybe this was fate.

After the service ended, as I walked out the front doors of the church, a tall, young man handed me a flier. At the top, in bold letters, it read, *WOMEN'S EVENT*.

A women's event? No way. That's not for me.

I'm not going, especially with "church" women. I shoved the flier into my purse without a second thought.

Selah

> "To those going through the valley and shadow of death, hear this word: Weeping will last through some dark, awful nights, and in that darkness, you will soon hear the Father whisper, 'I am with you. I cannot tell you why right now, but one day it will make sense. You will see it was all part of my plan. It was no accident.'" *David Wilkerson*

10

Praying Out Loud To God

Time passed. I moved on as if that weekend had never happened.

I should have been grateful. I should have been celebrating the fact that I survived an overdose and am alive. But I couldn't see past my mistakes. I couldn't see the miracle of it. Instead, I only saw my failure.

Unable to process everything, the trauma took over. It overshadowed the good — the prayers spoken over me and the times I made it to church.

My head and heart were in conflict. I was being torn apart inside, and eventually, I surrendered to the easier narrative: that everything was random and just a coincidence, despite the truth right in front of me.

Desperately wanting to change, I was terrified of what that would mean. I couldn't imagine living outside of the only lifestyle I knew. Instead of healing, I buried myself in doing what I knew best: making money. I slipped back into my old ways, but this time, I went all in — pushing myself to the extreme.

Before, I had worked two or three nights a week. Now, it was every night. Sometimes, I began as early as when the club opened at 11 a.m., staying until I exceeded my quota. Each day, I set a new goal for myself, determined to reach it no matter the cost. Money was my addiction and my worth.

Outside of work, I slept, ate out, shopped, and spent hours at the gym. I sculpted my body into the image I believed men wanted. On my computer, I studied pornographic images of women with long hair, heavy makeup, large breasts, and tiny waists — convinced that this was empowerment, the key to being validated.

There were no boundaries left, not inside the club or outside. I was fully immersed in the lifestyle of a full-time stripper. I didn't care how I was seen by others. I was entitled, proud, and convinced I had every right to be who I wanted to be. This went on for months, and eventually, I ran myself into the ground.

It took a toll on me—physically, emotionally, and spiritually. My body grew weary, and I became more intolerant of people, the club's environment, and the regime this entailed.

In the wider realm of California, the economy crashed and made the club's prices go up, so customers weren't spending as much. It even increased the house fees that the dancers had to pay out to the manager, the DJ, the door guy, and the house mom. Overall, the clientele spent less, were more demanding, and expected more for the dollars they offered.

Anxiety and hostility simmered in my attitude. The customers could sense it, and consequently, it showed in my earnings. I knew I needed a break, but I told myself I had to meet my predetermined goal every month. Previously, I would be excited to go to work, energized by the potential of how much I could earn. But after five years in the industry, and months of pushing myself harder than ever, that feeling faded. The glamour and glitz had worn off.

There were nights when I would pull into the parking lot and sit in my car, engine running, deep in thought. Conflicted feelings between going in or driving away tore me apart, but what would I do if I went home? I despised being alone. Maybe I'd call a friend and end up at a bar—something I was trying to avoid. So, I forced myself to go into the den of iniquity one more time.

One Friday night, I arrived later than usual. Turning off the engine, I struggled to calm myself by repeating positive affirmations out loud. Despite it, negative thoughts rushed in. My heart pounded in my chest, and I felt panic.

From the parking lot, I could hear the music blaring. I knew exactly which song was playing and who was on stage. I tried to gather the courage to get out, but I had no strength in my body. I couldn't do it. My mind told me I had no choice, that I had to work, because my rent and my car payment would be overdue.

Then, in that moment of crisis, I did something I hadn't done. *I prayed. I cried out —*

> "Dear God, I hate this place! I hate doing this. I have no strength to go on. Please protect me and help me find a way out. Thank you for listening. Amen."

What happened next was unlike anything I had ever experienced. A wave of supernatural peace flooded over me. I had never felt anything like it before Nurse Marisol, and I had never prayed out loud before. But at that moment, it was real. God was there with me.

It was the first time I cried out to God, and His presence left an indelible mark on my heart.

I knew, deep down, that He had heard me. That He was with me. And even though I ended up going into work that night, I was sure that God would answer me. My first step was to abstain from working on weekends anymore.

Selah

"When you call on me and come to me in prayer, I will listen to your every word. If you reach out to me, you will find me when you search for me with all your heart. I will not disappoint you," declares YAHWEH. "All that you have lost, I will restore, and I will gather you from all the nations where I have scattered you. I will bring you back home to the land from which I exiled you," declares YAHWEH. *Jeremiah 29:12-14, TPT*

11
Women's Event

One Saturday, as I rummaged through my purse, I stumbled upon a flier. It read, *"Women's Event."* It was the same flier handed to me when I visited that church.

Ironically, it happened to be the day of the event. At first, I was determined I wasn't going. But something nudged at me, almost pleading, and so, despite my resistance, I decided to check it out. As I walked into the foyer of the church, it was just as massive as I remembered it. A large sign with an arrow pointed me toward the women's event. Taking a deep breath, I forced a smile and walked in. There were several tables covered with pink tablecloths, and at the center of each table was a vase of fresh flowers.

Scattered across the tables were permanent markers and name tags. I found an empty table, the one closest to the hallway door. I sat down, grabbed a pen, and hesitated over what name to write on the tag. Should I use my real name, or would an alias be better? I was used to using fake names to hide my true identity.

Bravely, I wrote my real name. As I wrote it, more women began filling the room. To my surprise, four women sat at my table.

The event started with mingling, and everyone rose to grab light refreshments. There was coffee, tea, and water adorned with pretty flower petals and lemon slices. A long table was lined with muffins, scones, neatly cut sandwiches, and slices of cake. I had never attended a women's event before, but I couldn't help but be impressed by the decorations, and I enjoyed the food.

Everything was going well until it was time for introductions. We were prompted to go around the table and share a bit about ourselves, including what we were struggling with in this season of life.

As each woman spoke, I observed closely. The first person, a middle-aged woman, shared about her marital problems. She openly talked about going to counseling after discovering that her husband had cheated on her. I didn't know what to think. I felt guilty while my mind drifted to all the married men who came into my strip club.

The next woman was much younger than the first, probably my age or even younger. She was bubbly and bright, talking enthusiastically about her new baby. But as she spoke, there was a quiet sadness beneath her words. She was struggling with motherhood, feeling remorse for being away from her baby, and trying to juggle the new demands.

As she spoke about the highs and lows of motherhood, an intense pain hit me. I began to feel uncomfortable, my thoughts turning dark. I recalled the absence of my mother and her abandonment of me.

The lies whispered, **"You *are* unlovable. Unworthy."**

Doubts like a torrent flooded my mind. I felt condemned. How could I share my story here, surrounded by women who seemed to have their lives together? How could I tell them that I stripped for a living? How could I admit I worked at a gentlemen's club?

In an instant, I convinced myself I shouldn't be there. I didn't belong in that room, in that space of women sharing their struggles. I wasn't like them. I had nothing in common with them. I could never be accepted here. And, I have nothing to contribute.

Before I could stop myself, I interrupted, asking where the bathroom was. I excused myself, got up, and quickly made my way to the exit. I held back my tears as best I could, but as soon as I got to my car, I broke down. I sobbed, and the tears poured out uncontrollably.

At that moment, I believed I would never escape the adult entertainment industry. I felt completely ensnared. I had no way out. I had gotten so deep, so lost in it, that I could not see a future outside of its world. I realized I had nothing to show for myself — not the degree I once dreamed of, nor the goals I had set.

When was the last time I felt excited about something? The last time I allowed myself to dream? This was a new low. A darker place than I had ever imagined I would reach.

I regretted coming to the women's event. Wishing I had never set foot in that church. This was not a place where I belonged. The church was not for women like me.

I was done with church.

Selah

> "I called on your name, Lord, from the depths of the pit. You heard my plea: 'Do not close your ears to my cry for relief.'" *Lamentations 3:55–56, NIV*

12

God Leaves The 99 For The 1

My mind was made up. I would never go back to church or attempt to find a God who did not exist.

A coldness clenched my heart. I was done seeking, done trying to understand the supernatural experiences I had undergone earlier. Or attempt to find a god who did not exist. I didn't want to wrestle with it anymore or continue to feel tormented. I fully accepted who I was and the lifestyle I had chosen.

Dancing made my life better. It provided for me in ways I couldn't have achieved otherwise. I was living independently with the freedom to work whenever I *wanted*, buy whatever I *desired*, and travel wherever I *pleased*. So what if I didn't have a college degree; I was making more money than most people.

Aggressive workouts became a way to bury my pain. I pushed myself strenuously at the gym, aiming to achieve the "perfect" figure. This was the weapon I could use to manipulate the men to do whatever I asked, and my vengeance was to take their money and make them believe they had a chance with me, only to end up facing my rejection later. I hated men, and I felt justified in getting back at them. I convinced myself they deserved it, especially the ones who were married with families. Those disgusted me the most.

My life returned to the old normal. Customers were spending again, and I was back on top of the world.

After a few weeks off to travel, I returned to the club. That's when I first noticed them—a small group of women sitting in the corner.

"Do you know why those women are here?" I asked one of the other dancers.

"They say they are with God or something. They don't tip, but they give out cute gift bags."

Gift bags? Seriously? This is a strip club, not a sorority house, I thought to myself.

I was furious. They were being intrusive and disrespectful by being here. They had no business in a strip club! So, I ignored them.

They came back the next week and the week after that. They were persistent. I didn't understand why the other dancers treated them politely. I wasn't going to succumb to their kindness.

One night after my set, I walked around to collect my tips. The women were in their usual corner with gift bags. As I passed by, I heard a soft, but unmistakably clear, audible whisper.

"Stop."

It was distinct and made me stop in my tracks.

It was God's voice.

Looking up, I saw a woman with the kindest eyes, handing me a paper gift bag.

"We made this for you," she said gently.

Her warmth took me aback. Her demeanor was compassionate, and her voice was soft like the heavenly one I had just heard. Unsure of what to do with it, I went straight to the dressing room. Once I got there, I ducked into a bathroom stall and opened the gift bag. I don't remember if I thanked her as I took the bag, but curiosity filled me.

Inside was a small hand lotion, lip gloss, and a pocket-sized book of Psalms. I opened it and read the verses. They were like a balm to my soul, echoing my cries and struggles.

At that moment, I believed this wasn't a coincidence. Deep in my heart, I knew that God had been chasing me all along. He had heard my cries and answered my prayers. He was pursuing me after all.

He came here, even to a strip club, for me.

Selah

> "There once was a shepherd with a hundred lambs, but one of his lambs wandered away and was lost. So the shepherd left the ninety-nine lambs out in the open field and searched in the wilderness for that one lost lamb. He didn't stop until he finally found it." *Luke 15:4, TPT*

13
New Beginning

After that night, I began reading the Psalms booklet and praying every day. As I read the passages from King David's heart, I began to recognize my own struggles, sufferings, and longings reflected in his words. My heart and mind found comfort in them. For the first time in a long while, I didn't feel alone or abandoned.

Praying to God required learning something new. It was awkward and unfamiliar at first, but no matter what I said or how long I prayed, a sense of peace and clarity followed.

The next week, I went to work hoping to see the women again, but they didn't come. Would they return? I mulled. After my shift, I came home and looked through the gift bag they had given me. Inside, I found a white card stuck to the side. The card had their ministry name, contact information, and the days they invited women from the industry to attend a Bible study at their church. It planted a seed of desire to attend one of their meetings.

When I arrived, the room was full. The leader introduced herself as the founder of the ministry. She shared how she had once been an exotic dancer in Las Vegas before she encountered Jesus. Through her relationship with Jesus, her life had been completely transformed. I was inspired and hopeful that I, too, could change.

Through studying the Bible, God began to renew my mind and fill me with His Spirit. Slowly, I began working less at the club, limiting myself to just enough shifts to cover my essential bills.

I also started attending the same church. It was a mega church, and the pastor, a former NFL player, taught sermons that were inviting, interesting, and refreshing to my soul. He was open about his own struggles in the past, which made me feel safe enough to let down my guard at church.

During this time, I began praying to God for direction. I asked Him, "What are my next steps? How can I stop working at the club completely? What other jobs could I pursue? What changes did I need to make to leave this life behind?"

I realized that if I wanted to live with integrity and stability, I needed to go back to school full-time.

So, I began exploring different career pathways, wanting to pursue something meaningful. Nursing stood out to me, but in Southern California, the waiting lists were long. I considered applying to schools out of state, but then I struggled with how I could afford to support myself while attending school.

Once again, I felt mired in the muck of my previous choices.

But I kept praying. Then, one day, God told me I needed to move back home to the Midwest. I thought it was a huge request, but I was willing to do whatever it took to follow Jesus, even if it meant returning to a place that held such painful memories. God promised me He would always be with me wherever I went.

God began preparing me for this move. He taught me to be frugal and start saving. I began reaching out to Appa and my family. I told them how I was contemplating moving back and my plans to go to nursing school. At first, they were surprised and in disbelief. They thought I loved California, but they were also excited for me to come home. I kept in touch with Appa, regularly updating him on my progress. I heard loving support in his voice.

These small, but bold acts of faith were pivoting my life and marking a turning point. It gave me hope and was also the beginning of reconciliation with my family.

Selah

> "This means that anyone who belongs to Christ has become a new person. The old life is gone; a new life has begun!" *2 Corinthians 5:17, NLT*

14
Goodbye

It had been months since I last worked at the club. I had thrown away my outfits, my spare work heels, and even the last pair of shoes I had kept "just in case" I needed one more shift. When God impressed on my heart that I was not to work there anymore, I knew He was serious.

There was no turning back, no matter the reason, including what I defined as emergencies.

I had made a covenant with Him, a commitment far deeper and more valuable than a promise. I was going to follow Him now. He would direct my steps. This was the obedience He expected from me. On my part, it was an act of faith.

I had given my YES to Jesus, and within a matter of months, He had brought so much restoration to my life. He had lifted burdens I never thought possible, helping me to forgive others, even my family, from whom I once felt misunderstood and rejected. He brought me hope and joy.

It was His strength that helped me resist the temptation to go back to the club. At times, it felt like a tug of war, even a life-and-death struggle. After I took one big step forward, I'd find myself sliding three steps back, leaving me battered and defeated. It was spiritual warfare. Lies would taunt me, and I would retreat to my bed, feeling helpless and depressed.

A Bible remained close to my bed. With what little strength I had, I'd reach for it and open to Psalms again. The verses verbalized my soul's cries. The words covered my tender heart.

Fall came to Southern California, though the seasonal changes went by without notice. But I knew something had shifted. I was transforming, becoming a new and different person. For the first time, I looked to the future with hope and anticipation. I never thought I would want to leave California, but I knew the longer I stayed, the harder it would be to move and the greater the inclination to change my mind.

There was so much beauty here — the year-round warm weather, ocean views, tall palm trees, and access to the most amazing Mexican food.

A part of me would miss this place and the California vibe, but I knew I had to leave. I had to leave to become fully untethered from the strip club.

Coexisting with this feeling of fresh possibilities was a deep sadness. A loss by the sense of disconnection that would come from leaving behind the women I had met at the club, especially my dear friend, Starlight.

I knew leaving the adult entertainment industry would be interpreted as rejecting one world for a better one. I would be seen as a traitor. This would not hold me back; I had made a covenant with God. Additionally, I made arrangements with Appa, giving him a clear date for when I was leaving. He was expecting me. I was excited to start over again. This time, the right way.

I scheduled to meet Starlight at a park near my apartment. She had become less responsive lately, not messaging me like she used to. Was she angry? Hurt? Did she even care? I prayed she would show up. I wanted to see her one last time before I moved out of state.

It was twenty minutes past the time we were supposed to meet. I sat on the swing, waiting.

Then, in the corner of my eye, I saw a blue car. It was Starlight!

She parked, and I walked over to her. We gave each other the biggest hugs.

"I didn't think you would show up. I thought you had flaked on me," I said, overjoyed.

"I am the *BIGGEST* flake, but I wouldn't flake on you. You know I'm terrible at goodbyes," she said, groaning.

We both laughed hysterically, the tension between us easing.

I looked into her large brown eyes, those eyes with diamond specks of green I always admired.

"I don't want you to leave," she said, her voice filled with emotion.

"Sis, I know. But I can't live like this forever. God has a plan for me."

Starlight understood, but also didn't. She was puzzled.

"Are you gonna come back? Visit me at least?"

"I don't know. I just can't stay here. I'm too tempted to go back to the club. I want to be in school and get my degree."

For the next couple of hours, we stayed in the park, talking about life. We laughed, cried, and swore we would reunite when the time was right. I gently encouraged, spoke life into her, and reminded her of who she truly was — her true identity in Jesus. Not the false identities from the world. She let me pray for her, which was a huge step in her faith.

We hugged, snapped a few pictures, and went our separate ways.

A Note to Starlight

Dear Sis,

One day, I would come back for you. I would help you and others who long to leave the club find a way out.

I would tell you how much our heavenly Father loves you. How deeply He cares for you. He does now and always will. Nothing will ever stop Him from loving you or pursuing you.

Love,

Jihya

I didn't know it, but this would be the last time I saw Starlight. A few years later, I found out from a mutual friend that Starlight had passed away from an overdose. For years, I carried guilt and grief. During my healing process, I often wondered, how do I talk about this, especially when there is so much stigma in the world around women in the adult entertainment industry? Where can we have conversations in a safe space without judgment?

Like Starlight, there are many women who never leave the industry because the struggles to do so are insurmountable. The hurdles are high and complex. There is incrimination from others, self-harm, and so much more.

Selah

"The Spirit of the Sovereign Lord is on me, because the Lord has anointed me to proclaim good news to the poor. He has sent me to bind up the brokenhearted, to proclaim freedom for the captives and release from darkness for the prisoners, to proclaim the year of the Lord's favor and the day of vengeance of our God, to comfort all who mourn, and provide for those who grieve in Zion— to bestow on them a crown of beauty instead of ashes, the oil of joy instead of mourning, and a garment of praise instead of a spirit of despair. They will be called oaks of righteousness, a planting of the Lord for the display of his splendor." *Isaiah 61:1-3, NIV*

15
Baby Christian

I was on fire for God. As a baby Christian, I was ready to go wherever God wanted me to go and do whatever he called me to do. I wanted to be a missionary for God. I wanted to follow Him and share about Him.

The longer I stayed in California, the more eager I became to move away. The thought, the temptation to go back to the club for just one more night, was always there. I would pray incessantly, asking God to take those desires away. And, he helped reduce them. He reframed my mindset. I went from feeling stuck and stagnant to having an actionable plan for my next steps. This time, I saw a real future ahead of me, and I was ecstatic.

When God guided me to move back home, I didn't think twice about it. I didn't storm off or dispute it with Him like I normally used to do when I was upset. He softened my heart and helped me humble myself. I was learning that He knows what's best for us, even if he had to pluck me out of California. So, for me, the first step to a new life was to go back home.

I was going to live with Appa for an opportunity to study full-time, but I sensed there was more to it. God wanted to restore and reconcile my broken relationships with my family. He also wanted me to intercede to help mend some generational pains. When I asked Appa if I could come back home, it was an instant yes. He didn't ask any questions or analyze the plans I made. There were no harsh rules or set contingencies. Appa took me in with arms open wide. He was so happy that his daughter was home. He let me live with him rent-free and unconditionally. I knew he only wanted me to be comfortable and well-fed during nursing school.

Two years later, I was so proud to have earned a college education. The three letters BSN after my name were a dream come true. I was tremendously grateful because I deemed this opportunity to be a gift from God. For the first time, I was earning money in an honest and dignified way. No more lying about what I did for work or coming up with stories on how I earned my rent or paid for lavish trips. Whenever anyone asked what I did for work, my eyes would twinkle, my posture would straighten, and I would proudly say, "I'm a registered nurse."

It was my first academic milestone. Instantly, I felt the lies of my youth disappear. Lies that said I wasn't smart enough and would end up being a loser. This single victory meant so much more to me, knowing it was God's strength and transformative power. It helped me get through nursing school week after week, especially at the beginning of every semester when it felt like the faculty were putting a lot of pressure on the students and weeding them out.

It had been about three years since leaving the strip club. My degree and Jesus were a shield around me, preventing me from going back.

Selah

> "Forget the former things; do not dwell on the past. See, I am doing a new thing! Now it springs up; do you not perceive it? I am making a way in the wilderness and streams in the wasteland." *Isaiah 43:18-19, NIV*

16
Church Hurt

After nursing school, I found a megachurch quite similar to the one in California, where I committed my life to God. Following a long season of solitude and building a 1:1 relationship with Him, I was ready to grow my faith by joining a community of believers.

Although I attended services for quite some time, I still didn't feel plugged in or connected. In early spring, there was an announcement about an upcoming mission trip to an orphanage in Central America. My heart yearned to help the impoverished in remote places. I thought this was the perfect opportunity to serve and be used by God. I began praying about whether I should apply. There was a stirring in my spirit to go for it, so I did.

A few weeks later, I was notified that I had been accepted. This was another milestone in my walk of faith. I couldn't wait for this adventure and to share Jesus with others, especially in a part of the world that needed Jesus desperately.

The first meeting was held in a children's classroom. I walked in and saw a man in his late twenties grabbing chairs and setting them in a circle. Without asking, I jumped in and grabbed more chairs to help him.

He came over and, with a firm grip, shook my hand. "Hi, I'm Christopher, but call me Chris. I'm one of the team leads. Jamie is the other lead, but she always runs a little late," he said sarcastically.

"Hi, I'm Jihya," I replied, grinning from ear to ear.

"You're the first one to show up. We'll get started once the others arrive. Well, if they come," he said jokingly.

As I sat down, I looked over the questions I had written in my notebook. Soon, others came in, shook hands with Christopher, and sat down. There were eight others. All from different backgrounds, ages, and stages in faith.

Right away, Chris and Jamie introduced themselves and provided insight into the orphanage and the objectives for this mission trip. They discussed the orphanage's needs and what would be expected of us. Next, we went over the outline and what topics would be covered at each of the meetings before we travel overseas.

Eventually, the atmosphere shifted, and they discussed what was asked of the team members, such as rules, etiquette, and fundraising. Jamie then bluntly declared that there was to be no dating or PDA among team members on the trip. I thought it was a little strange that she emphasized this without giving any context and saying it abruptly.

The meeting went on for two hours. We were overloaded with information. By the end of the meeting, the excitement dissipated, and members expressed concerns, especially about costs and questions about what if they couldn't fundraise enough. The meeting wrapped up with the leaders assigning homework, including scripture memorization for the trip. Next, we were informed that we would be taking turns sharing our testimony. Jamie explained this was part of developing the team.

I had never shared my testimony with anyone before, especially in a group setting. The thought of questioning this never crossed my mind. I had just met the leaders, and they seemed like they knew what they were doing. The process sounded logical.

Others were expected to share, so I was willing to do my part.

The meetings were held every two weeks, and different team members shared their testimony each time. I tried not to compare. Many of them were raised in the church and had acknowledged Jesus at an early age.

My turn was approaching, and I spent time preparing and rehearsing what I would say. In prayer, I felt led by the Spirit to be completely honest and open in what I share. I felt confident and eager to describe how and where I encountered Jesus.

When the meeting came, I opened up by going straight into my story. I shared vulnerably and alluded that I was in a dark place, that I had hit rock bottom, and even attempted suicide. My story included descriptions of how I struggled with identity and disclosed that I had made a living by being an exotic dancer at a strip club. Eventually, I concluded with how God ultimately came to me by sending a group of women into my work, and that a gift bag they had given me changed the course of my life.

As I wiped away tears and came down from being nervous, I felt relieved, but when I saw all the blank stares, I started to question whether I had revealed too much. There was a moment of silence. The awkwardness stung.

Immediately, Christopher clapped and said, "Praise Jesus. That's great!"

I took my time leaving and waited around in case anyone had any words of encouragement or questions they wanted to ask about my testimony. The way it ended left me deflated and doubtful. It was my first time sharing my testimony, and I didn't know if this was normal. Was I being too sensitive? I wondered if what I shared was inappropriate.

A few days later, I got a text message from Drew, one of the guys on my mission team trip. Since I had never talked to Drew directly, I assumed he got my number from the group contact list. He asked me to come over to his house to work on an idea he had in mind for the kids at the orphanage. I didn't know him very well, except that he was about ten years older than me and divorced, which he had shared in the group. He seemed seasoned in his faith and was an active prayer leader at church. So when he invited me over to work on a project for the mission on the trip, I didn't hesitate to think anything of it.

It was my day off work, and around lunchtime. I rang his doorbell, and Drew opened the door. He greeted me in a t-shirt and baseball cap. I didn't recognize him at first; maybe because I'd never seen him outside of church or church attire, but something about his demeanor was different. Typically, he was reserved and kept to himself in the meetings, but now he was jovial and talkative.

When I got there, he had started grilling some burgers and hot dogs for us to eat. He offered me a plate, and I sat at his dining room table and ate. I listened and followed along in his stories. He bragged a lot about his online business and how it was soon going to launch. I looked at the time and realized nearly an hour had passed without talking about the mission trip. After another thirty minutes, I told him that I had to head home because I needed to prepare for my shift tomorrow morning at the hospital.

He insisted I stay a little longer. I didn't want to be rude, considering he made me lunch, so I said I could stay for just a bit longer.

He got up, put his dish in his sink, and then moved to his couch in the living room.

"Hey, I have something I want to tell you. I thought it was really bold of you to share your testimony. Not many people would do that."

Suddenly, the shift in his tone caught my attention. His words were also validating, because I had been feeling doubtful about sharing my testimony. He then proceeded to tell me that his past had a dark history, too. Looking proudly, he shared that he used to go to strip clubs and that many of the dancers would come home with him. He nonchalantly added that none of them could keep up with his sex drive.

My anxious misgivings changed to repulsion! His comments were inappropriate, and I felt extremely uncomfortable. With apprehensive dread, my heart beat rapidly, and I realized that I was isolated and alone with him. I wanted to tell him he was disgusting, but my mind was blown away, and my thoughts conflicted. How is this possible when he is a leader at church?!?

I thought he was a safe person.

Seductively, he tells me how he likes me, and then he leans forward and kisses me.

I didn't know what to do.

Automatically, my body freezes out of fear. The same familiar type of fear that I experienced when I was being molested as a child.

Drew presses himself on me.

He is forceful.

He continues to kiss me and doesn't stop there.

I am defenseless.

The Next Day

I was in a daze. My body was sore. I tossed and turned in bed, having little strength. Deceived. Betrayed. Blind sided to say the least. I felt used.

The abyss engulfed me, and the voice of suicide whispered my name. I had reached my lowest point again, remembering the last time I was in a similar state when I tried to commit suicide. This time, it was much more complicated and confusing because it involved someone of faith.

Unable to wrap my head around what happened, I couldn't say the 'R' word because it wasn't the typical scenario of rape, but it was definitely non-consensual!

Lies, shame, and guilt congregated within me.

I started to believe the falsehoods and thought it was my fault, which is often a guilt and burden many victims like myself think.

Then I became frantic and worried that I could contract an STD or possibly become pregnant. After calling in sick at work, I looked up pregnancy resource centers on my laptop, headed to the nearest location, and got screened.

Days later, I still hadn't received messages from Drew. It was as though a giant vacuum had sucked the whole event right out of reality, and it had never happened.

The day before our next mission meeting, he wrote me an email saying he was terribly sorry. He's regretful, but he has repented. He asks me to keep it a secret.

Repented? I don't know what that even means!

My internal whirlpool is spiraling out of control. I confided in a couple of the women in my group, and they offered their support, but I don't think they fully understood what actually occurred. They seemed to assume it was consensual. Do I say rape? But was it rape? I didn't fight back, and I wasn't drugged.

Satan was tormenting me and playing games with my mind. In the Bible, he is called the accuser, and he was playing that role in my head very strategically.

Out of desperation, I messaged Christopher, our leader, and told him I urgently needed to talk to him. After calling him, venting, and telling him everything, I thought he would express concern and caring, but he lashed out. He threatened to kick me off the team because there were strict rules about having sexual relations with team members. I tried to convey that we weren't in a relationship; how Drew forcibly came onto me, and I didn't know who to tell, but I needed help. Christopher wasn't listening. I got off the phone and realized he was hearing what he wanted to hear, and it dawned on me that he did not believe me.

Reflecting on my testimony and how he probably saw me as what I once was, a former stripper. I called up one of my girlfriends in the group and told her Christopher's responses. She was disappointed, but wasn't surprised. She told me that he was a fairly new believer and that he got his leadership role because of who he knew in the church. She shared that he had been radically saved and came out of a life of addiction. I was surprised because he didn't include that in his testimony.

A couple of weeks before the mission trip, I decided not to go, but after prayer, God told me to go after all. It was hard to pretend nothing happened. At times, I felt rage, especially whenever we prayed in a group setting and Drew led. I wanted to call him out in front of everyone. I wanted to rip out his eyes. A strong desire to tell others that he took advantage of me and of my vulnerability stuck in my mind. Didn't they see? He was a wolf dressed in sheep's clothing.

Throughout the mission trip, at the end of each day of attending to the children, I would go to a viewpoint near the orphanage and watch the sunset. Although the landscape was vast and barren, it was the only place I could put my guard down. I could trace the enormous mountains in the distance. Sitting on top of a boulder and taking in the scenery, I would release my true feelings. I suppressed everything until this part of the day. Crying out to God and journaling was how I ended most of my days.

Yet God felt distant. His presence wasn't near, and I couldn't hear his audible voice like I normally do.

I wrote in my notebook, *"God, why did you allow this to happen to me? Why does church hurt so much?"*

No answer came, and I felt abandoned. Utterly alone.

Then swiftly, the accuser came in again and dropped condemning thoughts into the void within my heart. The enemy of my soul warned me to never share my story again, or I would be taken advantage of and hurt once more.

The lies sounded like the truth.

Selah

> "The thief comes only to steal and kill and destroy; I have come that they may have life, and have it to the full." *John 10:10, NIV*

17

A Godless City

My soul was deeply wounded. That incident left me confused and wanting to run away. It made me not want to stay in the Midwest any longer. Perhaps God had brought me back for only a season, and now it was time for me to find a new path and move on.

My plan was to move as far away as possible. Because of my past, I couldn't go back to Southern California, but after visiting Portland, Oregon, for my birthday weekend, I sensed God directing me to relocate to this city.

After weeks of no contact, Drew somehow found out I was moving out of state. He sent me an email saying the news affirmed to him that we wouldn't have worked out since I was leaving. He also strongly advised against moving to Portland, calling it a "godless" city.

His email was offensive. How dare he contact me again? I could expose what happened and cause serious trouble for him, but at this point, I just wanted to forget and move on as far away from him and the church he represented. When I did speak out, no one believed me, leaving me isolated, dejected, and depressed.

He labeled Portland a "godless city." I had never heard anyone describe a city in such terms before. This upset me even more because it suggested that God ordains which places He favors and abandons others. That couldn't be true because God is everywhere. I wanted to write back to challenge his thinking and address free will, but the Holy Spirit convinced me to surrender it instead.

Still, his comment made me curious. I searched online for

information about Portland, Oregon. In a way, he was correct. Oregon was among the least religious states in the country. I kept scrolling and found another headline: "Portland, the city with the most strip clubs per capita in the United States."

No way, I thought.

A lack of churches and non-religious people, I could handle. Maybe, given what had happened, it would be better to stay away from churches and the members who called themselves "Christians." But the idea of moving to a city with the most strip clubs per capita? That statistic gave me pause and concern.

Was this from God's heart or the enemy's schemes? Was the deceiver leading me to a new city to isolate and quarantine me, in order to break me down and tempt me back into my old patterns of behavior?

Fervent prayer was required to assure myself of what God wanted me to do; He would make a way. But I also couldn't sit idly by expecting doors to magically open.

Later that day, before opening my daily devotions, I bowed in prayer, laying my requests before God. I told Him I was broken again and in need of His full protection. I was fearful and vulnerable.

When I finally opened my devotional, the verse at the top of the page read:

> "Whether you turn to the right or to the left, your ears will hear a voice behind you, saying, 'This is the way; walk in it.'" Isaiah 30:21, NIV

God's supernatural peace washed over me as I read that passage. I felt Him reassuring me — "I will be with you every step of the way."

It assured me that if I made the wrong choice, He would redirect me. I made a two-year plan in which, if things didn't go well, I would enroll to be a travel nurse. But staying where I was had become unbearable, and I wasn't healing. The very next day, I applied for my Oregon nursing license. As soon as I became a registered nurse in that state, I would book a one-way flight to Portland.

Selah

> "Whether you turn to the right or to the left, your ears will hear a voice behind you, saying, 'This is the way; walk in it.'" *Isaiah 30:21, NIV*

18

Portland

Portland, a place so green and with such fresh mountain air, felt as though I was breathing for the first time — each inhale was more revitalizing to my spirit. My senses were awakened, and I was hypnotized by the novelty of living in a new city. Once again, I was living alone in a one-bedroom apartment close to downtown, but this time, I was a young healthcare professional, no longer defined by my past.

Feeling free again and being in a new space allowed my heart to mend. Downtown Portland was vibrant and bustling, each block teeming with artisan shops offering unique handmade crafts, mom-and-pop restaurants serving only organic, farm-raised ingredients, and trendy coffee shops filled with hipsters, writers, and book lovers.

"This," I thought, *"is my place."*

Every adventure left me feeling small in the grace-filled grandeur surrounding me. I visited every park, standing in awe beneath towering evergreen trees, sensing a majestic presence. It was as if I could visualize God once again, as if the whole world was new and fresh again. As I explored every part of the city — the hidden corners, the lively streets, even the areas marked by brokenness and chaos I saw God's heart and fingerprints, no matter how far people had strayed from Him.

Strolling through the Saturday street markets, I sensed His provision and plans, drawing me deeper into the city. I was captivated. When I passed by strip clubs, I wasn't enticed or repulsed. God's protection enfolded me in all new ways.

I didn't yet fully understand what He was doing, but in my

spirit, I knew there was a good reason.

"Trust Me", I felt Him whisper. *"Someday, you will understand."*

For now, I was away from painful memories and other distractions. I wasn't sure if God wanted me to stay in Portland long-term, but I yearned to plant deep roots despite having nothing to anchor me.

In the months that followed, I would come to understand what it truly meant to be consecrated, set apart, while fighting off temptations and resisting the pressures of the world. It was not easy, to say the least.

During that season, I slowly made my way back to church. I found a congregation that held evening services, which fit my night shift schedule. Having never seen so many young hipsters in one gathering for a moment, I felt out of place. To my surprise, the lead pastor looked like a misfit himself. He was dressed casually in a denim jacket and ripped jeans, a stark contrast to the polished church leaders I had known before. Yet, his theology was sound, deeply rich, and spoken with meekness and compassion. He shared openly about his struggles with depression and anxiety, making him relatable, almost *human*.

His words sparked something in me, offering a radical perspective on what it meant to truly follow Jesus. It resonated deeply because I had felt that same conviction when I left the adult entertainment industry. After walking away from that life, all I wanted was Jesus. That was the reason I was here. Tenderly but persistently, God was drawing me into a season of wilderness to be with Him and Him alone.

Selah

"Where you go, I will go." *Ruth 1:16, NIV*

19
Perfect Love

My deepest yearning was to feel loved. As a little girl, I dreamed of one day finding my "one and only". He would whisk me away, and we would make our home in the land of happily ever after, forever. It mattered not the city or type of dwelling we lived in. What was of most importance was that we were together, and that would be enough for my happiness.

It was insignificant what our occupations were, either. If we had to work odd jobs or put in long hours, we would always come home to each other. Our residence would be our refuge from the outside world. In my romanticized image, I envisioned lots of natural sunlight, freshly picked flowers in a vase somewhere, yummy home-cooked meals, and intimate, cozy spaces to dream and rest together.

In my dreams of marital love, it was always pure, light, honest, unconditional, and forgiving, no matter the circumstances. Unfortunately, in all my previous relationships, it was the exact opposite. I had experienced only a shallow, superficial version of love—a counterfeit.

After a failed marriage and several relationships, I realized none of them were the real thing. I was a broken person trying to use another broken person to make me whole. With everything I had gone through and done, I knew if I was ever to remarry, it would require a very special person to see past my failures and love me for myself, to love the parts that I was ashamed of and afraid to expose to the light.

But little did I know that in order for me to ever truly love someone else or receive love fully, I had to learn what perfect love is: God's love.

In 1 Corinthians 13, verses 4-8 NIV, it says,

"Love is patient, love is kind. It does not envy, it does not boast, it is not proud. It does not dishonor others, it is not self-seeking, it is not easily angered, it keeps no record of wrongs. Love does not delight in evil but rejoices with the truth. It always protects, always trusts, always hopes, always perseveres. Love never fails."

God's love is the exact opposite of everything I knew and had learned from the world. After leaving the adult entertainment industry, it took me a long time to fully comprehend this love and the great sacrifice He made because of his perfect love.

When I finally began to grasp this, there were weeks when I wept spontaneously. For the first time, my heart was being convicted of all the things I had done. I had lived most of my life feeling and acting like a victim, but I was as guilty as some of the perpetrators. During this time, I made confessions and allowed the Holy Spirit to interject. He worked at purifying and softening my heart so I could be compassionate to others and myself.

Selah

"Perfect love casts out fear." *1 John 4:18, NIV*

20
Bo

Thoughts of whether I should go or not spun in my mind on a continuous conveyor loop. Thirty minutes before our scheduled date, I knew I had to decide quickly. I had woken up long past my alarm because working nights had turned my sleep into a rollercoaster ride. Finally, I rallied enough energy to get out of bed and commit to going. If it didn't go well, at least I could say I had tried dating and now I could put it behind me.

I rinsed my face, applied light makeup, and slipped into an oversized sweatshirt, leggings, and moccasin boots. Lately, I have worn baggy clothing on dates to avoid sending the wrong message. I have standards now and want to set clear boundaries.

Online dating has been a disaster thus far. How did people do it regularly? Every conversation felt shallow and meaningless. I quickly learned that listing "Christian" or "faith" on a profile meant nothing. When I asked about their spiritual life and beliefs, I received a variety of responses, ranging from "I go to church on holidays," "My family is religious," or even "I don't remember putting that on my profile."

When I talked about Jesus, the mood always shifted. Before meals, I would ask my date to pray, and when he refused or hesitated, I bowed my head and prayed alone. More often than not, I would end up splitting the check. Was this what dating as a believer looked like?

Some friends suggested broadening my search by removing the faith filter, saying I might stumble upon someone who was growing in their faith. It was tempting, but I couldn't do it.

My hope dwindled. If finding someone with a personal relationship with Jesus was impossible, then I would be happy remaining single.

Then, out of nowhere, I received a free month's trial on a Christian dating site. I was skeptical of all dating apps by then, but the offer was free. What did I have to lose? I gave myself one last month.

By the third week, I was ready to quit. I had gone on one date, and it had been a long shot. Frustrated, I went into my account settings, prepared to deactivate my profile. But before I did, I prayed out loud: "Lord, if You want me to get married, please help me find a husband. Otherwise, I will remain single for you, God. In Jesus' name, Amen."

The next day, I received a notification of a new match.

Excited, I opened his profile only to feel disappointed. He wasn't my type.

How could I pursue marriage if I wasn't attracted to the person? But what if this was God answering my prayer? I felt a nudge from the Holy Spirit and decided to message him.

The Date

It was a chilly November evening, and the rain poured heavily. I rushed out the door, running several blocks to the cocoa shop where we had planned to meet. My moccasins were soaked, and I was already twenty minutes late. I should have just canceled.

Frustrated, drenched, and breathless, I entered the shop. I spotted him instantly — glasses, quiet demeanor, patiently waiting. He hadn't ordered a drink yet. Across from him sat an empty chair, waiting for me.

Apologizing profusely for being late, I sat down. I could tell I was talking too fast — a telltale sign of nerves. He smiled, assured me it was fine, and offered to buy me a warm drink.

His name, Toby. He explained that this was his middle name and what he went by when he was at work. When he was home with his family, they called him Bo. Bo fit him perfectly.

He was kind. Meek, but strong. Instantly, I felt seen and safe.

The conversation flowed easily. He was genuinely curious and engaging. We unraveled layers of how we saw ourselves, two different worlds intersecting at this point in time. He had grown up in Oregon, and the majority of his family still lived in the area. Several years after college, he moved back to his childhood home to help care for his mother after she suffered a stroke. His parents were still married after 40 years, and he considered them his friends. He and his dad shared a love for movies.

Bo was a pastor's kid. His family once held church services in their home, where he had worked the property like a farm. His father baptized people in their courtyard hot tub while his mother worked full-time and would bake desserts for their Sunday services. His life was stable, grounded, and totally the opposite of mine. Yet, we shared the same intense love for Jesus.

Then he revealed something unexpected: He had waited his entire life for a wife. He had remained pure. I would be his first girlfriend. His first kiss.

He worried that most women wanted someone experienced. For me, this was a breath of fresh air. I was used to men wanting to take sexual advantage of me as quickly as possible.

The next day, we met again for an impromptu second date. We attended church together and grabbed a bite to eat. When our food arrived, I asked Bo to pray. Nervously, he stumbled a bit over his words but prayed anyway. It was the confirmation I needed.

As we spent more time together, I knew I had to share my past. My testimony. I was terrified. Would he think I was unfit to possibly be his wife? Would I lose him?

We set aside a night to exchange our spiritual journeys with God. He went first, sharing his prior struggles with anxiety, anger, and even pornography. There was nothing he held back, and it was clear that he didn't fit the perfect submissive or rebellious pastor's kid stereotype. He was simply Bo.

Then it was my turn.

I told him everything: my abusive marriage, how I entered the adult entertainment industry to escape it, and how I became trapped in it, eventually hit rock bottom, and attempted suicide. Then, finding Jesus when a group of women appeared at my club to show me I was loved, and God rescued me from the pit I was in.

Bo didn't flinch. He didn't pull away in disgust. His eyes filled with tears, and he squeezed my hand. "I'm so grateful for what God did," he said. "I don't think less of you."

Then he asked something no one else had ever dared to ask me, "Were you sexually abused as a child?"

For the first time, I shared my childhood abuse and also how I was taken advantage of by a church leader after sharing my testimony. With Bo, my secrets came into the light, and I experienced a new level of healing and freedom.

Then he made me a promise: "I will always protect you."

Ten months later, in a beautiful vineyard, his father officiated our wedding. We both said, "I do." It was the best day of our lives.

After ten years, God had redeemed the image and meaning of marriage for me, and it was only the beginning.

Selah

> "Love is patient, love is kind. It does not envy, it does not boast, it is not proud. It does not dishonor others, it is not self-seeking, it is not easily angered, it keeps no record of wrongs. Love does not delight in evil but rejoices with the truth. It always protects, always trusts, always hopes, always perseveres. Love never fails." *1 Corinthians 13:4–8, NIV*

21

Daughter, Share Your Story

For many years, I compartmentalized my faith. I didn't feel safe telling my testimony or openly talking about God. Even in church, there were unspoken norms about what was acceptable to share and unspoken rules on how God should be presented. Sometimes, the world and the church looked much too similar. Instead of transforming to be more like Jesus, I found myself conforming to church culture.

In those church circles, I held back my most vulnerable stories out of self-protection. If I shared it with women, they might judge me. If I shared it with men, they might see me differently, as if I were "easy."

Outside of church, I was no different. We lived in Portland, Oregon, a city known for its low religious affiliation. I feared people would see my beliefs as radical, rigid, or even laughable. Other people's opinions of me still continued to shape what I did and said.

I called myself a Christian. This is what I am supposed to be, right? My life was together, and I wasn't rocking any boats. But in reality, I had become the very thing I despised — a lukewarm believer. My passion for Jesus faded when I stopped depending on Him and instead placed my trust in worldly things.

A Time of Reflection

When the coronavirus pandemic hit in 2020, everything changed. The world shut down. Churches, once considered safe havens, were closed. Services moved online. Everything felt uncertain and confusing. During that season, I began to examine my faith and the broader church culture more critically.

Was church truly a safe place? Was it as welcoming as it claimed to be?

In my experience, it often felt like some people had "executive-level memberships," while others were just regular attendees with no special access. I questioned church leadership. Were they truly shepherding people? Was the body of believers hungry for God? Based on my limited exposure to church, the answer for me was "No".

And as I looked deeper, I saw my own shortcomings coming to light.

I longed for genuine community with other believers, yet I also felt relief when church was no longer in person. Having grown weary of small talk and superficial connections, I began to wonder what the church would look like if every single participant truly embodied heaven on earth.

A New Church and a New Beginning

After a long break in 2023, my family and I visited the English service at a Korean Presbyterian church. Everyone, including the pastors, was welcoming.

At first, we weren't sure if it would become our home church. The drive was nearly an hour each way, the denomination was different, and I had never imagined myself attending a Korean church. My personal associations with Korea were complicated, and as a Korean American woman, I often felt inadequate in my own identity.

But week after week, God kept leading us back. We joined a small group and started serving. We felt seen for the first time in a long time. Making connections was effortless, and slowly my heart began to heal.

A few months in, my husband, Bo, and I had the opportunity to share our testimonies with our small group. Leading up to that night, I reflected on the first time I had shared my story in a similar setting. I knew this experience would be different; this time, my husband would be beside me. But more than anything, I felt convicted. Hiding parts of my story no longer seemed truthful.

I wanted to model transparency and vulnerability, just as Jesus did. However, in a Korean community where shame and saving face are deeply ingrained, I knew that sharing openly would be a powerful act of faith.

After I finished my testimony, Pastor Daniel affirmed me as God's beloved daughter. I saw Angie, his wife, and other women in my group wiping away tears. That moment, when others cried with me, when they felt the weight of my pain and lifted me up with encouragement, was a glimpse of the Father's heart.

For so long, I had struggled with my identity as a Korean American woman, with the shame of my past, and with the fear of sharing my testimony. That day, God redeemed it all. It was a profound, transformative milestone — the key to unlocking a deeper level of healing.

It was also the beginning of something bigger.

A Call to Share

Later that year, in early fall of 2023, the Holy Spirit placed a strong impression on my heart: *"Now is the time to share your story."* Not in five years. Not in ten years. Now. I recognized His call, but I was terrified. Lord, I'm not ready yet. In truth, I don't think I ever will be. It had been locked away for years and wanted to stay that way.

I gave God a list of reasons why I couldn't do it. Including being a mother and a healthcare professional. What if people at my son's school found out his mom used to be a stripper? What if it affects my career? Nurses can be incredibly judgmental.

Worst of all, what if my Korean family shunned me? How can they know about what I did during those years I lived in California?

The stakes felt too high.

I convinced myself that I would share my story someday, but not now. Give it some time still. Just like that, I thought I was in the clear. However, God had other plans, and only a few days later, He whispered, *"Daughter, share your story."*

I knew it was Him, and yet, I still resisted.

That night, I tossed and turned. I couldn't sleep. Waking up in the middle of the night, I knew I wouldn't have peace about my decision.

"Why, God? Why now?" I asked. But there was no immediate answer.

The Vision

Later that week, while doing the dishes, I had a vision. Due to the intensity and distinctness, I knew it could have only come from God.

I saw a woman lying on a cold, bare floor. Darkness surrounded her. Demons tormented her, whispering lies, tempting her to take her own life. She was helpless. Defenseless.

At first, I thought it was a memory from my past, but God made it clear. It wasn't me. This woman was someone else—someone out there struggling to leave the adult entertainment industry but unable to break free.

That image shattered me. I couldn't wash the dishes anymore. Breaking down, I could only weep.

It convicted my heart, exposing my blind spots - my pride, my need for control, and my misplaced identity.

I had forgotten what God had done for me. Forgotten that He went to the strip club for me. But in that moment, I also remembered that God is everywhere and *He goes to dark places.*

He leaves the 99 for the 1.

I would not be where I am today if it weren't for Jesus. Right now, I could still be trapped in an abusive relationship. Perhaps I might never have left the industry if God had not come to me at my club.

Everything I am, everything I have, is because of Him.

He gets all the glory.

Believing that truth again made the risks seem smaller. They no longer felt so daunting, and I knew without a doubt that He would be with me every step of the way. I still didn't know how, when, or where to start sharing my story or what would come out of it.

The very next day, I saw a post by an online magazine called (in)courage that announced: "Share your story!"

I knew the invitation was from God, and it would be a

significant test of my obedience.

Selah

"You have come to your royal position for such a time as this." *Esther 4:14, NIV*

22

Strange Things

Strange things are happening.

People might think we're crazy if they hear us — especially if they hear me talk about the dead birds that have crossed my path. They would assume I'm exaggerating or making it up. But it happened twice in one week.

The mind tries to rationalize illogical situations, but I am certain this was no coincidence. I saw what I saw. It frightened me, making me realize what happens when you provoke the enemy. Actively pursuing others to come to God by sharing your story of redemption is the exact opposite of what satan wants. He is a thief. He comes only to steal, kill, and destroy.

Our lives are normal. My husband and I live in a safe bubble, far from crime and homelessness, out in the countryside with his parents. Our shared property, surrounded by tree nurseries and berry fields, carries a divine presence. Bo's father, a former pastor, once held church services in the house where he grew up. Baptisms were a regular occurrence in their courtyard.

It was a little after 9 a.m. the day after I submitted my story when, in my mind, I began forming a ministry catered to women in Portland's strip clubs. The thought excited me. I would be reaching out to those who have a similar story to mine in the same way others did for me. But, as badly as I wanted to jump on this new idea, I needed to get some work done that day and headed out for an appointment. We live on a long road, and as I was driving, I spotted something in the distance — a dead bird, its body sprawled across the pavement. I had just passed the perimeter of our property and that of our neighbor, who is also a believer. The carcass lay directly outside our property line.

It was a huge black bird, possibly a crow. Other birds surrounded it, pecking at its flesh.

Living in the countryside, we are used to seeing birds in the trees, but that morning, this felt different. There was something eerie about them; something dark. A chill ran through me.

Later that week, I left my work at the hospital and took the same path I always do to reach the main building. Suddenly, I nearly stepped on something — another dead black bird.

I gasped, jumping back. My heart pounding, I sprinted inside rushing into the closest bathroom. My hands shook as I dialed my husband's number. It went straight to voicemail.

What could this be???? I was horrified.

Remembering John 10:10: "The thief comes only to steal and kill and destroy..." But then, the rest of the verse echoed in my mind: "I have come that they may have life and have it to the full."

The enemy was trying to shake me. It was working, but I couldn't let him win.

I prayed, and in that moment, I felt God's presence and protection come over me. I didn't want to feel alone, so I confided in a few close friends who are believers about what we were doing and how I felt called to reach women in the adult entertainment industry.

Their responses caught me off guard. It was discouraging.

"Those people are really broken."

"Maybe you should wait until your children are older before getting involved in something like this."

Others warned me about the city's dark forces and principalities I would be up against. They told me about the Shanghai Tunnels and their dark history of sex trafficking.

I was disheartened, but I was not shaken. So, I persisted because God had promised His provision. He assured me that He would provide everything: the resources, the strength, and above all, the protection.

Since I first started this mission, opposition and fear have followed even from those closest to me. There were sudden attacks; my family began experiencing sickness. Some common ailments were headaches with no explanation or oppressive thoughts.

Turning to Bo, I asked, "Why are these strange things happening?"

"It's because we're in a spiritual battle," he calmly said. He adds, "For we do not wrestle against flesh and blood, but against the rulers, against the authorities, against the cosmic powers over the present darkness, against the spiritual forces of evil in the heavenly places (Ephesians 6:12 ESV)."

"So how do we fight?"

"You start by putting on the full armor of God."

He began teaching me about the unseen dark spiritual forces at work in this world, and my eyes opened to a whole new realm.

He also gave me this scripture: *"I have given you authority to trample on snakes and scorpions and to overcome all the power of the enemy; nothing will harm you." – Luke 10:19*

That verse became my sword and my shield.

I went from vaguely believing in spiritual warfare to fully believing in it and the power of God's word to fight against it. His words are my shield. Once I recognized the enemy's schemes, his attacks became predictable like clockwork. They always happened the week we planned to visit the strip clubs to prevent us from going.

If the enemy couldn't reach me or keep me silent, he would go after those closest to me.

Month after month, I learned how to prepare for battle. My prayers grew stronger. I asked others to intercede for myself, my family, and the women and men in the adult entertainment industry. I fasted weekly and fed on God's word daily.

After four months of visiting strip clubs with just my husband, I realized this ministry wouldn't be sustainable the way we were doing it. What if something happens with me inside while Bo is outside the parking lot? Though my in-laws helped with childcare, God made it clear that this ministry eventually would be led by women. It would take spiritually strong women to overturn the adult entertainment industry in our city.

I continued sharing my testimony, just as God asked me to do. All the while, I prayed for helpers. By spring, two women reached out, ready to volunteer. Two women whom I had never met before, but were very specific and hand picked. Women who had a pure servant's heart and were ready for battle.

God's vision was unfolding before my eyes. He was building a ministry team — just as He said He would.

Selah

"For we do not wrestle against flesh and blood, but against the rulers, against the authorities, against the cosmic powers over the present darkness, against the spiritual forces of evil in the heavenly places." *Ephesians 6:12 ESV*

23
Grandma

Grandma's shortness of breath had been worsening for some time.

Supplemental oxygen had been sustaining her, but when we received the news that her condition was no longer treatable and that breathing treatments would no longer help, it was only a matter of time before she would be with the Lord.

After a long day in the emergency department, Grandma was admitted to a small hospital room, where we would say our goodbyes.

When I arrived to visit her, I wasn't surprised to find that even in her final hours, Grandma remained unapologetically herself. She was still lifting others up, still being the bright light she had always been. Her charm, witty humor, and powerful prayers encouraged everyone who came into her room, including the hospital staff.

I will never forget the impact she made on my life.

When I was dating Bo and first introduced to his Grandma, something happened that none of us could explain. She broke down in tears, and no one, not even Grandma, understood why. Later, after Bo and I got married, he would joke that I was the one who made Grandma cry.

A few months before her hospitalization, I had written my testimony for (in)courage. Grandma was one of the first people I shared it with before it went public. I was nervous and eager to hear her thoughts, but when we spoke, I could feel the radiance of joy flow through the phone as she praised me and told me how proud she was.

Then, she *paused*. Her voice softened, and she said something I will never forget: She now understood why she cried when we first met. It was because God had made an impression on her heart, showing her that I was safe. Safe from harm. Free from the dark places I had once been. She told me she had always sensed that I had lived through something dark, even without knowing the specifics. She never needed me to say it.

I broke down in tears on the other end of the phone. This time, I was the one crying — as tears of joy streamed down my face.

While on the phone, I thought about how foolish it was that I hadn't shared this part of my life with her sooner. But I also realized how powerful shame can be. It keeps us locked in the dark, hiding parts of our stories and keeping them secret.

I'm so grateful I had the chance to tell her before she passed.

Even in her final days, lying in her hospital bed, fading in and out of consciousness, I wasn't sure how much Grandma could hear. But when I told her all about how God was building a ministry to reach women in the strip clubs right here in our city, she became alert, gave me her full attention, blessed me, and thanked God for His hand at work.

Grandma became the biggest cheerleader for my ministry. If she could, she would have come with me to visit the clubs. She loved people with an unshakeable force, not judging anyone by their past or their choices - just like Jesus. She saw each woman as His beautiful and precious daughters.

Grandma was the embodiment of salt and light in this world. Her love and compassion for others reflected the light of Christ in everything she did.

Selah

"You are the *salt* of the earth. But if the salt loses its saltiness, how can it be made salty again? It is no longer good for anything, except to be thrown out and trampled underfoot.

You are the *light* of the world. A town built on a hill cannot be hidden. Neither do people light a lamp and put it under a bowl. Instead, they put it on its stand, and it gives light to everyone in the house. In the same way, let your light shine before others, that they may see your good deeds and glorify your Father in heaven." *Matthew 5:13–16, NIV*

24
Salt + Light Ministry

To be continued.

Acknowledgements

To my dearest husband, Bo,

Thank you for choosing me every single day. Your love and support have been my refuge as I've worked through telling the hardest chapters of my life. Thank you for encouraging me to share my story unapologetically and for always standing beside me.

To my sweet boys,

You are my life's biggest blessing and greatest joy. Thank you for teaching me the depth of unconditional love. May you always know that your true identity is found in God and continue to share His light with the world. I am always praying for both of you.

To my beloved in-laws, Micheal and Renee,

Thank you for loving me as if I were your own daughter. Your example of humble servanthood has left a lasting mark on our family legacy. I'm deeply grateful for your genuine love and unwavering support—especially for walking beside me every step of the way as I shared my testimony and served God through Salt + Light Ministry.

To the brightest grandma, Arlene,

I miss you dearly. I felt God's love radiate through you so clearly. Thank you for loving me unconditionally from the moment we met, and for being with me in spirit during every outreach—even from heaven. Though you're no longer physically with us, your presence is deeply missed, and your love and humor will remain a cherished part of my heart.

To pastors Daniel Lee & Ai Nitta,

Thank you for your faithful care for those who are often unseen, forgotten, and marginalized in society. Your tangible support to Salt + Light Ministry has planted many seeds of hope and is helping advance God's kingdom in Portland, Oregon. I am tremendously grateful for both your constant obedience and partnership with our Heavenly Father in this important work.

Thank You

Dear Reader,

I want to thank you for reading my book. There are countless other books, yet you chose mine. That means more to me than words can express, and I'm truly honored.

As you read these words, I'm imagining you wherever you are—whether at home, in a break room at work, a coffee shop, an airport, or somewhere else where God's presence begins to fill the space. I pray that His love will transcend through the pages of my story and that it will feel tangible to you.

This book is a compilation of some of the parts of my life that God has redeemed. It's not complete, because He is still writing my story, just as He is still writing yours. These chapters offer a glimpse into my past and show the brokenness and fragility of my heart before I truly knew Jesus.

During the writing process, I felt a distinct impression from God to highlight certain chapters of my past. Full disclosure, I was terrified to expose those publicly because I thought they were too "dirty."

For much of my life, even after becoming a follower of Jesus, I believed that sharing certain stories was too risky—especially within the church. I feared rejection, criticism, and shame, even from fellow believers. But those fears became barriers to my own spiritual growth.

For years, I contemplated the risks. I made many excuses to God, telling Him it wasn't worth it. But running in circles, consumed with these thoughts, became an exhausting way to live. Eventually, I ran out of steam. I grew tired and realized I didn't want to run anymore.

Within the four chambers of my heart, I kept a tender story—one too heavy to bear alone, yet waiting for the "right time" to be shared.

From my experience, when stories are surrendered to God's light, darkness flees, and Jesus makes a way for:

Hope

Healing

Comfort

Meaning

Freedom

These things made the risks worth taking. I did it for God, and for the women who have endured similar experiences, to remind them that they are never alone.

I pray that you start to believe that what we've done, or the horrific things others have done to us, do not define us or form our identity. They hold no power over our present or future. The only power they have is the power of Jesus when we invite Him in.

What He did for me, He will do for you too. Jesus is a real Savior who redeems and transforms lives—especially when we are willing. His love is free and always readily available.

I pray that my story brings hope and light into your darkness, no matter what circumstances you've faced or what hidden stories you carry.

If my story has touched you or you have enjoyed it, please consider leaving a review to help get it recommended to others.

With His love,
Jihya

About the Author

Jihya Harris's life is a powerful testament to God's redemptive love. Her story of being pursued by God in the unlikely setting of a gentlemen's club proclaims the truth that no place is too dark for His presence.

Born in Busan, South Korea, Jihya immigrated to the U.S. at a young age and grew up wrestling with her identity as a Korean American woman. Before encountering Jesus, she carried deep wounds of abandonment and shame, especially around her story. Today, she boldly shares her testimony so that other women might discover the same freedom and hope she found.

Jihya is a wife, mother, registered nurse, writer, evangelist, and advocate for vulnerable women. She and her family live just outside Portland, Oregon, a city known for having the most strip clubs per capita. When she is not caring for patients or ministering through Salt + Light Ministry, she loves sipping coffee, hosting women's gatherings, chasing spontaneous adventures, and finding rest in cozy corners of her home with her family.

If you like to say hello to her, please email her at wesaltlight@gmail.com or find her on IG @salt_lightministry. Please don't be a stranger — she'd love to hear from you!

Salt + Light Ministry

Salt + Light is a boots-on-the-ground ministry that shines God's light in some of the darkest places of Portland: strip clubs. We are led by women from diverse backgrounds, including lived experience in the adult entertainment industry. We are committed to meeting adult industry workers where they are, sharing the love of Jesus, and offering resources, support, and discipleship. Our mission is to champion every sister, no matter where she is on her journey with Jesus.

Stay connected @salt_lightministry

Endorsements

"I'm honored to call Jihya my friend. She is one of the most genuine, courageous, inspiring, and uplifting people I know — passionately committed to helping free and empower other women from captivity through the name of Jesus."
— Ai Nitta, English Ministry Pastor of Bethel Presbyterian Church

"Jihya Harris speaks truth, loves authentically without hidden motives, and is devoted to setting the captives free. She brings healing to those held in bondage. Through her faithful testimony, she opens doors for others to encounter God's transformative love, bringing restoration to communities."
— Julie Nowacki, State Director of She Leads Oregon

"Even from just a sample, I was hanging on every word—emotionally invested, mentally stirred, and spiritually impacted. Jihya Harris doesn't shy away from the hard realities of life. Instead, she faces them head-on, allowing the reader to sit in the tension of joy and sorrow, hope and disappointment, love and loss.
Her writing weaves seamlessly between past and present, giving real-time insight into how childhood trauma and cultural experiences shape a person's life. As a fellow survivor of both the sex industry and domestic violence, her story felt strikingly relatable. I found myself reflecting deeply, not just on her journey, but on my own. She educates and evokes empathy naturally. Through moments of heartbreak, suspense, and beauty, Harris captures the fragile, fleeting connections of humanity in a way that lingers long after you stop reading. "
— Faith Casey, Founder & Executive Director, Light of Love Ministries

"Jihya's story is a powerful testament to grit, strength, and surrender. In her journey to take control of her life, she discovers that true freedom comes when we let God take the reins. No story is too dark, no life too broken for the Lord to redeem—and Jihya's willingness to let Him do that work, not just for herself but for

others, will inspire you to rise, heal, and believe again."
– Katie Mathews, Limitless Journey CEO, Author, Motivational Speaker, Life Coach

"Jihya Harris's memoir is one of the most raw, courageous, and redemptive stories I have read. From the very first line, I was captivated by her vulnerability, her strength, and the aching truth she carries so bravely through every page. Her journey is not just one of surviving domestic violence and reclaiming her voice—it's a sacred invitation for all of us to examine the places where we've felt powerless, ashamed, or unseen.
This is not just a memoir. It's a testimony. A reminder that even at our lowest, we are never beyond the reach of grace. Jihya's words carry the weight of lived experience and the hope of someone who has found purpose through pain. I am deeply honored to endorse this book—and even more honored to call Jihya a sister in the journey toward healing and wholeness.
Her story will stay with you long after you've turned the final page—and it just might lead you to your own turning point."
– Megan Babcock, RN, BSN, Board-Certified Holistic Nurse and Trauma-Informed Coach, Best Transformational Coach in Oregon 2025, Founder of It's Your Story to Tell

"Jihya's memoir powerfully exposes the deception and damage of the adult entertainment industry. With raw honesty, she shares her journey through broken dreams to redemption and healing. A must-read for those seeking truth and hope."
– Joni Wilkinson, Founder & Executive Director of One's Purpose, an anti-trafficking organization.

"Jihya's vulnerable generosity is found in these pages. Her story is a tender offering that will illuminate hope for many who feel alone in the dark."
– Tasha Jun, author of Tell Me the Dream again

"A good story keeps you on your toes, eagerly anticipating how it will unfold — and Jihya's story is no exception. These pages will draw your heart and mind back to the Author of all authors, reminding you in a powerful and undeniable way that Jesus is always at work (including YOU reading this right now). Jihya's journey will leave you in awe of God's relentless pursuit and His boundless love. This

book is an absolute must-read!"
— Krista Breilh, Founder of Live Salted

"In a world that often tells us we're too broken, too far gone, or too hidden to be redeemed, God Goes to Dark Places is a much-needed reminder of who God really is. Jihya has written this book beautifully, weaving her personal experiences with deep biblical truth to show that there is no place too dark for God's light to reach. He is not afraid of the places we think He won't go—He meets us there, offering a new life, a second chance, and a fresh start. If you've ever felt unseen, unworthy, or beyond redemption, this book will remind you of the relentless love of God and His power to transform even the darkest of places into something beautiful."
— Hope Reagan Harris, 3x author, podcast host, and Founder of the Purpose Doesn't Pause Movement

"Jihya's story is powerful—it gives hope to those who feel stuck in dark places, believing there's no way out. Knowing her now, many years later, she carries light, joy, and freedom to everyone she meets. She is constantly pursuing those who feel trapped, helping them find the way."
— Christine Hong, Owner of Abba Coffee Roasters

"Jihya's story will go places to your heart in ways you wouldn't expect. It's more than an engaging journey of healing and redemption out of a dark time; it's an artfully woven description of life's vulnerability that might resonate with readers in ways they haven't processed yet in their own minds and hearts. God is going to work through her life story to bring hope and break chains of bondage for others and set the captives free!"
— Robyn McLean, Speaker & Writer, Founder of Stirring Embers, Owner of Brewed GRIT

"Jihya is as much of a leader in her life as she is in her words. She's not afraid to go into the subjects and topics we tend to shy away from in society and the church. Her story of returning to The Father after trying life her way is vulnerable, compelling, and inviting. I believe that this story will reach those who have wandered from God, or those who have never had the chance to encounter His love. Her words are personable and relatable. This story is a gift to women and this world.

– Lily P. McLaughlin, Safe Spaces

"I honor Jihya, who unfolds an honest and bold testimony told with vulnerability and courage about an industry filled with shame and rejection."
– Amy Ahn, Film Producer

"I am so honored and grateful to have Jihya as a friend and colleague in ministry. Her story is truly inspirational and unlike any that I've ever heard. She is one of the most genuine and selfless people that I know. The first time I heard her share her story, I couldn't believe all the things that she had experienced throughout her life. What was even more amazing was that through it all, Jihya had kept such a loving and kind Spirit, which I suspect had been there all along. She is so authentic and confident in who she is, and her core desire is to give God the glory in every aspect of her life. God Goes to Dark Places is such a raw and vulnerable retelling of her life. Every word, every part of it, weaves such a beautiful and honest picture of her journey. Throughout the book, Jihya does such a wonderful job navigating both her Korean and American identities, giving respect to all the people and places along the way that shaped her and made her who she is today. Readers also get such a wonderful example of her almost real-time prayers and honesty with God, even in the darkest moments of her life. And what Jihya has found is what I hope all readers will find, and that is a renewed sense of hope and faith in God's plan and timing for all things."
– Daniel Lee, Bethel Presbyterian Church English Ministry Pastor